WUTHERIN

Love is not always a happy experience. Nor do people who love each other always treat each other gently. We are all familiar with stories where two lovers are kept apart by outside forces – sometimes by their families, sometimes by the customs of their society.

In *Wuthering Heights* the main force that keeps the lovers apart is themselves. The characters in this story, just like real people, have weaknesses – and their weaknesses lead them into unhappiness. They are proud and selfish; they often have mixed feelings and are unable to make up their minds. For these reasons love often fails, but rarely as passionately and dramatically as in this story.

OXFORD BOOKWORMS LIBRARY
Classics

Wuthering Heights

Stage 5 (1800 headwords)

Series Editor: Jennifer Bassett
Founder Editor: Tricia Hedge
Activities Editors: Jennifer Bassett and Alison Baxter

EMILY BRONTË

Wuthering Heights

Retold by
Clare West

OXFORD UNIVERSITY PRESS

OXFORD
UNIVERSITY PRESS

Great Clarendon Street, Oxford OX2 6DP

Oxford University Press is a department of the University of Oxford
It furthers the University's objective of excellence in research, scholarship,
and education by publishing worldwide in

Oxford New York

Auckland Bangkok Buenos Aires Cape Town Chennai
Dar es Salaam Delhi Hong Kong Istanbul Karachi Kolkata
Kuala Lumpur Madrid Melbourne Mexico City Mumbai Nairobi
São Paulo Shanghai Saipei Tokyo Toronto

ISBN 0 19 423075 9

This simplified edition © Oxford University Press 2000

Seventh impression 2004

First published in Oxford Bookworms 1992
This second edition published in the Oxford Bookworms Library 2000

A complete recording of this Bookworms edition of *Wuthering Heights*
is available on cassette ISBN 0 19 422792 8

Illustrated by Caroline Church

Typeset by Wyvern Typesetting Ltd, Bristol
Printed in Spain by Unigraf s.l.

CONTENTS

PEOPLE IN THIS STORY

MR LOCKWOOD'S STORY, 1801 TO 1802

At Thrushcross Grange
  Mr Lockwood, the narrator
  Ellen Dean, the housekeeper

At Wuthering Heights
  Mr Heathcliff, the landlord of Thrushcross Grange
  Mrs Cathy Heathcliff, a widow and Mr Heathcliff's
    daughter-in-law
  Hareton Earnshaw
  Joseph, a servant
  Zillah, a housekeeper

ELLEN DEAN'S STORY, 1770 TO 1802

  Mr Earnshaw
  Hindley Earnshaw, his son
  Catherine Earnshaw, his daughter
  Heathcliff, a gipsy boy
  Frances, Hindley's wife

  Mr and Mrs Linton
  Edgar Linton, their son
  Isabella Linton, their daughter

  Hareton, Hindley Earnshaw's son
  Cathy, Edgar Linton's daughter
  Linton, Heathcliff's son

  Joseph, a servant
  Ellen Dean, a servant
  Zillah, a housekeeper

CHAPTER 1

Mr Lockwood visits Wuthering Heights

1801 — I HAVE JUST returned from a visit to my landlord, Mr Heathcliff. I am delighted with the house I am renting from him. Thrushcross Grange is miles away from any town or village. That suits me perfectly. And the scenery here in Yorkshire is so beautiful!

Mr Heathcliff, in fact, is my only neighbour, and I think his character is similar to mine. He does not like people either.

'My name is Lockwood,' I said, when I met him at the gate to his house. 'I'm renting Thrushcross Grange from you. I just wanted to come and introduce myself.'

He said nothing, but frowned, and did not encourage me to enter. After a while, however, he decided to invite me in.

'Joseph, take Mr Lockwood's horse!' he called. 'And bring up some wine from the cellar!' Joseph was a very old servant, with a sour expression on his face. He looked crossly up at me as he took my horse.

'God help us! A visitor!' he muttered to himself. Perhaps there were no other servants, I thought. And it seemed that Mr Heathcliff hardly ever received guests.

His house is called Wuthering Heights. The name means 'a windswept house on a hill', and it is a very good description. The trees around the house do not grow straight, but are bent by the north wind, which blows over the moors every day of the year. Fortunately, the house is strongly built, and is not damaged even by the worst winter storms. The name 'Earnshaw' is cut into a stone over the front door.

1

Mr Heathcliff and I entered the huge main room. It could have been any Yorkshire farmhouse kitchen, except that there was no sign of cooking, and no farmer sitting at the table. Mr Heathcliff certainly does not look like a farmer. His hair and skin are dark, like a gipsy's, but he has the manners of a gentleman. He could perhaps take more care with his appearance, but he is handsome. I think he is proud, and also unhappy.

We sat down by the fire, in silence.

'Joseph!' shouted Mr Heathcliff. No answer came from the cellar, so he dived down there, leaving me alone with several rather fierce-looking dogs. Suddenly one of them jumped angrily up at me, and in a moment all the others were attacking me. From every shadowy corner in the great room appeared a growling animal, ready to kill me, it seemed.

'Help! Mr Heathcliff! Help!' I shouted, trying to keep the dogs back. My landlord and his servant were in no hurry to help, and could not have climbed the cellar steps more slowly, but luckily a woman, who I supposed was the housekeeper, rushed into the room to calm the dogs.

'What the devil is the matter?' Mr Heathcliff asked me rudely, when he finally entered the room.

'Your dogs, sir!' I replied. 'You shouldn't leave a stranger with them. They're dangerous.'

'Come, come, Mr Lockwood. Have some wine. We don't often have strangers here, and I'm afraid neither I nor my dogs are used to receiving them.'

I could not feel offended after this, and accepted the wine. We sat drinking and talking together for a while. I suggested visiting him tomorrow. He did not seem eager to see me again, but I shall go anyway. I am interested in him, even if he isn't interested in me.

* * *

2

Two days later Yesterday afternoon was misty and bitterly cold, but I walked the four miles to Wuthering Heights and arrived just as it was beginning to snow. I banged on the front door for ten minutes, getting colder and colder. Finally Joseph's head appeared at a window of one of the farm buildings.

'What do you want?' he growled.

'Could you let me in?' I asked desperately.

He shook his head. 'There's only Mrs Heathcliff indoors, and she won't open the door to you.'

Just then a young man appeared and called me to follow him. We went through the back door and into the big room where I had been before. I was delighted to see a warm fire and a table full of food. And this time there was a woman sitting by the fire. She must be Mrs Heathcliff, I thought. I had not imagined my landlord was married. She looked at me coldly without saying anything.

'Terrible weather!' I remarked. There was silence.

'What a beautiful animal!' I tried again, pointing to one of the dogs that had attacked me. She still said nothing, but got up to make the tea. She was only about seventeen, with the most beautiful little face I had ever seen. Her golden wavy hair fell around her shoulders.

'Have you been invited to tea?' she asked me crossly.

'No, but you are the proper person to invite me,' I smiled.

For some reason this really annoyed her. She stopped making the tea, and threw herself angrily back in her chair. Meanwhile the young man was staring aggressively at me. He looked like a farm worker, but seemed to be part of the family. I did not feel at all comfortable. At last Heathcliff came in.

'Here I am, sir, as I promised!' I said cheerfully.

'You shouldn't have come,' he answered, shaking the snow off his clothes. 'You'll never find your way back in the dark.'

'Perhaps you could lend me a servant to guide me back to the Grange?' I asked.

'No, I couldn't. There aren't any servants here except Joseph and the housekeeper. Get the tea ready, will you?' he added fiercely to the young woman. I was shocked by his unpleasantness.

We sat down to eat. I tried to make conversation with the three silent people round the table.

'How happy you must be, Mr Heathcliff,' I began, 'in this quiet place, with your wife and —'

'My wife! My wife's ghost, you mean?'

I suddenly realized I had made a serious mistake. So his wife was dead! Of course he was too old to be married to that young girl. She must be married to the young man next to me, who was drinking his tea out of a bowl and eating his bread with unwashed hands. Perhaps the poor girl had found no one better to marry in this uninhabited area. I turned politely to the young man.

'Ah, so you are this lady's husband!' This was worse than before. His face went red, and he seemed only just able to stop himself hitting me. He muttered something I could not hear.

'Wrong again, Mr Lockwood,' said Mr Heathcliff. 'No, her husband, my son, is dead. This,' he added, looking scornfully at the young man, 'is certainly not my son.'

'My name is Hareton Earnshaw,' growled the young man.

We finished our meal in silence, and when I looked out of the window, all I could see was darkness and snow.

'I don't think I can get home without a guide,' I said politely. No one answered me. I turned to the woman.

'Mrs Heathcliff,' I begged, 'What can I do? Please help me!'

4

'Take the road you came on,' she replied without interest, opening a book. 'That's the best advice I can give.'

'Mr Heathcliff, I'll have to stay here for the night!' I told him.

'I hope that will teach you not to walk over the moors in bad weather,' he answered. 'I don't keep guest bedrooms. You can share a bed with Hareton or Joseph.'

I was so angry with them all that I could not stay there a moment longer, and rushed out into the darkness. I saw Joseph by the back door, caught hold of the lamp he was carrying, and ran with it to the gate. But the dogs chased after me and attacked me, and I was soon knocked to the ground. Heathcliff and Hareton stood at the door, laughing, as I shouted at the dogs and tried to get up. In the end I was again rescued by the housekeeper, Zillah, who ordered away the dogs and helped me to my feet.

I was so bruised and exhausted that I did not feel strong enough to walk home, and although I did not want to, I had to spend the night at Wuthering Heights. Nobody wished me goodnight, as Zillah took me upstairs to find a bed for me.

CHAPTER 2

Catherine Earnshaw's room

1801 'QUIETLY, SIR!' WHISPERED the housekeeper, as we climbed up the dark stairs. 'My master will be angry if he discovers which bedroom you're sleeping in. For some reason he doesn't want anyone to sleep there, I don't know why. They're strange people in this house, you know. Here's the room, sir.'

But I was too tired to listen. 'Thank you, Zillah,' I said, and, taking the candle, I entered the room and closed the door.

The only piece of furniture in the large, dusty bedroom was a bed, placed next to the window. There were heavy curtains which could be pulled around it, to hide the sleeper from anyone else in the room. Looking inside the curtains I saw a little shelf full of books, just under the window. I put my candle down on the shelf, and dropped thankfully on to the bed. I closed the curtains around the bed, and felt safe from Heathcliff and everyone else at Wuthering Heights.

I noticed that there were names written on the wall in childish handwriting — Catherine Earnshaw, Catherine Heathcliff and Catherine Linton. Then I fell asleep, but I was woken very suddenly by a smell of burning. My candle had fallen on to a Bible on the shelf and was burning it. When I opened the Bible to see if it was damaged, I found that wherever there was an empty page, or half a page, someone had written on it, and on the first page was written 'Catherine Earnshaw's diary, 1776'. Who was the girl who had slept in this bed, written her name on the wall, and then written her diary in the Bible, twenty-five years ago? I read it with interest.

'How I hate my brother Hindley!' it began. 'He is so cruel to poor Heathcliff. If only my father hadn't died! While *he* was alive, Heathcliff was like a brother to Hindley and me. But now Hindley and his wife Frances have inherited the house and the money, and they hate Heathcliff. That horrible old servant Joseph is always angry with Heathcliff and me because we don't pray or study the Bible, and when he tells his master, Hindley always punishes us. I can't stop crying. Poor Heathcliff! Hindley says he

6

is wicked, and can't play with me or eat with me any more.'

My eyes were beginning to close again and I fell asleep. Never before had I passed such a terrible night, disturbed by the most frightening dreams. Suddenly I was woken by a gentle knocking on the window. It must be the branch of a tree, I thought, and tried to sleep again. Outside I could hear the wind driving the snow against the window.

But I could not sleep. The knocking annoyed me so much that I tried to open the window. When it did not open, I broke the glass angrily and stretched out my hand towards the branch. But instead, my fingers closed around a small, ice-cold hand! It held my hand tightly, and a voice cried sadly, 'Let me in! Let me in!'

'Who are you?' I asked, trying to pull my hand away.

'Catherine Linton,' it replied. 'I've come home. I lost my way!' There seemed to be a child's face looking in at the window.

Terror made me cruel. I rubbed the creature's tiny wrist against the broken glass so that blood poured down on to the bed. As soon as the cold fingers let go for a moment, I pulled my hand quickly back, put a pile of books in front of the broken window, and tried not to listen to the desperate cries outside.

'Go away!' I called. 'I'll never let you in, not if you go on crying for twenty years!'

'It *is* almost twenty years!' replied the sad little voice. 'I've been out here in the dark for nearly twenty years!' The hand started pushing through the window at the pile of books, and I knew it would find me and catch hold of me again. Unable to move, I stared in horror at the shape behind the glass, and screamed.

There were rapid footsteps outside my bedroom door, and then I saw the light of a candle in the room.

'Is anyone here?' whispered Heathcliff. He could not see me

I rubbed the creature's tiny wrist against the broken glass.

behind the curtains, and clearly did not expect an answer. I knew I could not hide from him, so I opened the curtains wide.

I was surprised by the effect of my action. Heathcliff dropped his candle and stood without moving, his face as white as the wall behind him. He did not seem to recognize me.

'It's only your guest, Lockwood,' I said. 'I'm sorry, I must have had a bad dream and screamed in my sleep.'

'To the devil with you, Mr Lockwood!' growled my landlord. 'Who allowed you to sleep in this room? Who was it?'

8

'It was your housekeeper, Mr Heathcliff,' I said, quickly putting my clothes on. 'And I'm angry with her myself! No one can sleep in a room full of ghosts!'

'What do you mean?' asked Heathcliff, looking suddenly very interested. 'Ghosts, you say?'

'That little girl, Catherine Linton, or Earnshaw, or whatever her name was, must have been wicked! She told me she had been a ghost for nearly twenty years. It was probably a punishment for her wickedness!'

'How dare you speak of *her* to *me*?' cried Heathcliff wildly. But as I described my dream, he became calmer, and sat down on the bed, trembling as he tried to control his feelings.

'Mr Lockwood,' he said finally, brushing a tear from his eye, 'you can go into my bedroom to sleep for the rest of the night. I'll stay here for a while.'

'No more sleep for *me* tonight,' I replied. 'I'll wait in the kitchen until it's daylight, and then I'll leave. You needn't worry about my visiting you again either. I've had enough company for a long time.'

But as I turned to go downstairs, my landlord, thinking he was alone, threw himself on the bed, pushed open the window and called into the darkness. 'Come in! Come in!' he cried, tears rolling down his face. 'Catherine, do come! My darling, hear me *this* time!'

But only the snow and wind blew into the room.

How could my dream have produced such madness? I could not watch his suffering any more, and went downstairs.

I waited in the kitchen until it was light enough outside for me to find my way through the deep snow back to Thrushcross Grange. The housekeeper there, Ellen Dean, rushed out to welcome me home. She thought I must have died in the previous

9

night's snowstorm. With a warm fire, and a hot meal, I began to recover from my unpleasant experiences.

After my stay at Wuthering Heights, I thought I would never want to speak to any human being again, but by the end of the next day I was beginning to feel lonely. I decided to ask Mrs Dean to sit with me after supper.

'How long have you lived in this house?' I asked her.

'Eighteen years, sir. I came here early in 1783 when my mistress was married, to look after her. And when she died, I stayed here as housekeeper.'

'Who was your mistress?' I asked.

'Her name was Catherine Earnshaw,' she replied.

'Ah, my ghostly Catherine,' I muttered quietly to myself.

'She married Mr Edgar Linton, a neighbour,' added Mrs Dean, 'and they had a daughter, Cathy, who married Mr Heathcliff's son.'

'Ah, so that must be the widow, young Mrs Heathcliff at Wuthering Heights!'

'That's right, sir. Did you see her? I looked after her as a baby, you know. How is she? I do want to know.'

'She looked very well, and very beautiful. But I don't think she's happy.'

'Oh, poor thing! And what did you think of Mr Heathcliff?'

'He's a rough, hard man, Mrs Dean. But I'm very interested in him. Tell me more about him.'

'Well, he's very rich, of course, and mean at the same time. He could live here at Thrushcross Grange, which is a finer house than Wuthering Heights, but he would rather receive rent than live comfortably. But I'll tell you the whole story of his life, as much as I know, that is, and then you can judge for yourself.'

CHAPTER 3

*Ellen Dean's story – Catherine
and Heathcliff as children*

———— WHEN I WAS a child, I was always at Wuthering
1770   Heights, because my mother was a servant with the
————   Earnshaw family. They are a very old family who have
lived in that house for centuries, as you can see from their name
on the stone over the front door. I grew up with Catherine and
Hindley Earnshaw, and we three played together as children.

One day, their father Mr Earnshaw came back from a long
journey. He had travelled sixty miles to Liverpool and back on
business, and was very tired.

'Look what I've brought you!' he told us all, unwrapping
something he was holding carefully in his arms. Catherine and
Hindley were expecting presents, and they rushed eagerly to see
what it was. They were very disappointed to see only a dirty,
black-haired gipsy child.

'I found him all alone in the busy streets of Liverpool,' Mr
Earnshaw explained to them, 'and I couldn't leave him to die.
He can sleep in your room.' But Hindley and Catherine were
angry because they had not received any presents, and refused to
let the strange child share their room. However Mr Earnshaw
insisted, and little by little the boy became accepted by the
family. He was called Heathcliff, as a first and last name. No
one ever discovered who his parents had been.

Catherine and he became great friends, but Hindley hated
him, and was often cruel to him. Old Mr Earnshaw was
strangely fond of this gipsy child, and frequently punished his
son for behaving badly to Heathcliff. Hindley began to be

11

jealous of his father's feelings for Heathcliff, and saw them both as enemies.

This situation could not last. As Mr Earnshaw grew old and ill, Heathcliff became even more his favourite, and Hindley often quarrelled with his father. When Hindley was sent away to study, I hoped that we would have peace in the house. But then it was that old servant Joseph who caused trouble. He tried to persuade his master to be stricter with the children, and was always complaining that Heathcliff and Catherine did not spend enough time studying the Bible or attending church services.

Catherine was a wild, wicked girl in those days. We had to watch her every moment of the day, to stop her playing her tricks on us. She was proud, and liked giving orders. But she had the prettiest face and the sweetest smile you've ever seen. I could forgive her anything when she came to say she was sorry.

She was much too fond of Heathcliff, and the worst punishment we could invent was to keep her separate from him. Her father could no longer understand her or her behaviour, and Catherine did not realize that his illness made him less patient with her.

At last Mr Earnshaw found peace. He died quietly in his chair by the fire one October evening in 1775. The night was wild and stormy, and we were all sitting together in the big kitchen. Joseph was reading his Bible at the table, while Catherine had her head on her father's knee. He was pleased to see her so gentle for once, and she was singing him to sleep. I was glad the old gentleman was sleeping so well. But when it was time to go to bed, Catherine put her arms round her father's neck to say goodnight, and immediately screamed, 'Oh, he's dead, Heathcliff! He's dead!'

Heathcliff and I started crying loudly and bitterly too. Joseph told me to fetch the doctor, so I ran to the village, although I knew it was too late. When I came back, I went to the children's room, to see if they needed me, and I listened for a moment at their door. They were imagining the dead man in a beautiful distant place, far from the troubles of this world. And as I listened, crying silently, I could not help wishing we were all there safe together.

CHAPTER 4

Catherine Earnshaw gets to know the Lintons

———— HINDLEY CAME HOME for his father's burial. What
1775 was more surprising was that he brought a wife with
———— him. She was called Frances, a thin, pale woman with a frequent cough. Now that Hindley was the master of the house, he ordered Joseph and me to spend our evenings in the small back-kitchen, as we were only servants, while he, his wife and Catherine sat in the main room. Catherine and Heathcliff were treated very differently. Catherine received presents, and could continue her lessons, but Heathcliff was made to work on the farm with the men, and, as a farm worker, was only allowed to eat with us in the back-kitchen. They grew up like two wild animals. Hindley did not care what they did, as long as they kept out of his way, and *they* did not care even if he punished them. They often ran away on to the moors in the morning and stayed out all day, just to make Hindley angry. I was the only one who cared what happened to the two poor creatures, and I was afraid for them.

One Sunday evening they were missing at bedtime, and Hindley ordered me angrily to lock the front door. But I did not want them to stay out in the cold all night, so I kept my window open to look out for them. In a while I saw Heathcliff walking through the gate. I was shocked to see him alone.

'Where's Catherine?' I cried sharply.

'At Thrushcross Grange, with our neighbours the Lintons,' he replied. 'Let me in, Ellen, and I'll explain what happened.' I went down to unlock the door, and we came upstairs very quietly.

'Don't wake the master up!' I whispered. 'Now tell me!'

'Well, Catherine and I thought we'd just walk to the Lintons' house. We wanted to see if Isabella and Edgar Linton are punished all the time by *their* parents, as *we* are.'

'Probably not,' I answered. 'I expect *they* are good children and don't need to be punished.'

'Nonsense, Ellen! Guess what we saw when we looked in at their sitting-room window? A very pretty room, with soft carpets and white walls. Catherine and I would love to have a room like that! But in the middle of this beautiful room, Isabella and Edgar Linton were screaming and fighting over a little dog! How stupid they are, Ellen! If Catherine wanted something, I would give it to her, and she would do the same for me. I would rather be here at Wuthering Heights with her, even if I'm punished by Joseph and that wicked Hindley, than at Thrushcross Grange with those two fools!'

'Not so loud, Heathcliff! But you still haven't told me why Catherine isn't with you?'

'Well, as we were looking in, we started laughing at them so loudly that they heard us, and sent the dogs after us. We were about to run away, when a great fierce dog caught Catherine's

14

leg in its teeth. I attacked it, and made it let go of her leg, but the Lintons' servants appeared and caught hold of me. They must have thought we were robbers. Catherine was carried unconscious into the house, and they pulled me inside too. All the time I was shouting and swearing at them.

' "What a wicked pair of thieves!" said old Mr Linton. "The boy must be a gipsy, he's as dark as the devil!" Mrs Linton raised her hands in horror at the sight of me. Catherine opened her eyes, and Edgar looked closely at her.

' "Mother," he whispered, "the young lady is Miss Earnshaw, of Wuthering Heights. I've seen her in church occasionally. And look what our dog has done to her leg! It's bleeding badly!"

' "Miss Earnshaw with a gipsy!" cried Mrs Linton. "Surely not! But I think you must be right, Edgar. This girl is wearing black, and Mr Earnshaw died recently. It must be her. I'd better put a bandage on her leg at once."

' "Why does her brother Hindley let her run around with such a companion?" wondered Mr Linton. "I remember now, he's the gipsy child Mr Earnshaw brought home from Liverpool a few years ago."

' "He's a wicked boy, you can see that," said Mrs Linton. "And did you hear the bad language he used just now? I'm shocked that my children heard it."

'I was pushed out into the garden, but I stayed to watch through the window. They put Catherine on a comfortable sofa, cleaned her wound and fed her with cakes and wine. I only left the house when I was sure she was well taken care of. She's a breath of fresh air for those stupid Lintons. I'm not surprised they like her. Everybody who sees her must love her, mustn't they, Ellen?'

'I'm afraid you'll be punished for this, Heathcliff,' I said sadly.

And I was right. Hindley warned Heathcliff that he must never speak to Catherine again, or he would be sent away from Wuthering Heights, and it was decided that Catherine would be taught to behave like a young lady.

She stayed with the Linton family at Thrushcross Grange for five weeks, until Christmas. By that time her leg was fine, and her manners were much better than before. Frances Earnshaw visited her often, bringing her pretty dresses to wear, and persuading her to take care of her appearance, so that when she finally came home after her long absence, she almost seemed a different person. Instead of a wild, hatless girl, we saw a beautiful, carefully dressed young lady.

When she had greeted all of us, she asked for Heathcliff.

'Come forward, Heathcliff!' called Hindley. 'You may welcome Miss Catherine home, like the other servants.'

Heathcliff was used to being outside all day, and had not bothered to wash or change his clothes. His face and hands were black with dirt. In spite of this, Catherine was very glad to see him and rushed up to kiss him. Then she laughed.

'How funny and black and cross you look! But that's because I'm used to Edgar and Isabella, who are always so clean and tidy. Well, Heathcliff, have you forgotten me?'

But, ashamed and proud, the boy said nothing, until suddenly his feelings were too much for him.

'I won't stay to be laughed at!' he cried, and was about to run away, when Catherine caught hold of his hand.

'Why are you angry, Heathcliff? You ... you just look a bit strange, that's all. You're so dirty!'

She looked worriedly at her hands, and her new dress.

'You needn't have touched me!' he said, pulling away his hand. 'I like being dirty, and I'm going to be dirty!'

16

As he ran miserably out of the room, Hindley and his wife laughed loudly, delighted that their plan to separate the two young people seemed to be succeeding.

The next day was Christmas Day. Edgar and Isabella Linton had been invited to lunch, and their mother had agreed, on condition that her darlings were kept carefully apart from 'that wicked boy'. I felt sorry for poor Heathcliff, and while the Earnshaws were at church, I helped him wash and dress in clean clothes.

'You're too proud,' I scolded him as I brushed his black hair. 'You should think how sad Catherine is when you can't be together. And don't be jealous of Edgar Linton!'

'I wish I had blue eyes and fair hair like him! I wish I behaved well, and was going to inherit a fortune!'

'He has none of your intelligence or character! And if you have a good heart, you'll have a handsome face. Who knows who your parents were? Perhaps a king and queen, far more important than the Lintons!'

In this way I encouraged Heathcliff to have more confidence in himself. But when the Earnshaws and the Lintons arrived back from church, the first thing Hindley did was shout at Heathcliff.

'Get out of my sight, until we've finished eating! I'll pull that long hair of yours if you don't obey me at once!'

'It *is* long,' said Edgar. 'I'm surprised he can see anything.'

This was too much for Heathcliff. He looked desperately around for a weapon, picked up a bowl of hot soup and threw it at Edgar, who started screaming. Hindley immediately took hold of Heathcliff and pushed him upstairs.

'I'm sure Hindley's going to hit him!' cried Catherine. 'I hate it when Heathcliff is punished! It's your fault, Edgar, you

17

He picked up a bowl of hot soup and threw it at Edgar.

annoyed him! Why did you speak to him?'

'I didn't,' replied Edgar, tears in his eyes. 'I promised Mother I wouldn't. I spoke *about* him, not *to* him.'

'Well, don't cry,' said Catherine with scorn. 'You've made enough trouble already. Here comes my brother.'

Hindley returned, hot and breathless.

'That'll teach him!' he said. 'And now let's have lunch!'

18

The others seemed to forget Heathcliff, but I noticed Catherine could not eat much, and I knew she was sorry for her friend. In the evening there was music from a travelling band, and dancing in the main room. Catherine said the music sounded sweeter from high up, and so she went to sit in the dark on the stairs. When I went to find her, however, I discovered she had gone right to the top of the house to talk to Heathcliff through his locked bedroom door, and had then climbed out on to the roof and in through his window. I persuaded them both to come out of the room the same way, as I had no key to the door, and took Heathcliff down into the warm servants' kitchen with me, while Catherine returned to her guests and the dancing.

'You must be hungry, Heathcliff,' I said. 'You haven't eaten all day. Have some Christmas cake, do.'

'I can't eat anything,' he growled, putting his head in his hands. 'I've got to think how I can have my revenge on Hindley. I only hope he doesn't die first! He'll be sorry he's treated me like this, Ellen!'

CHAPTER 5

Catherine and Edgar

IN THE SUMMER of this year Hindley's wife Frances 1778 had her first, and last, baby. They called the boy Hareton. But the poor woman had been ill for a long time, although we had not realized it, and died soon after Hareton was born.

Hindley only had room in his heart for two people, himself

and his wife, so when she died, he was in despair. He neither cried nor prayed. Instead he swore at God and man, and drank himself to sleep every night. The servants all left him, except for Joseph and me. Joseph enjoyed being able to scold his wicked employer, with warnings from the Bible, and I could not leave Miss Catherine. After all, I had grown up with her and Hindley.

But the master's behaviour was a bad example for Catherine and Heathcliff. At fifteen, Catherine was the most beautiful girl for miles around, but she was proud and quick-tempered. She led what was almost a double life. At Wuthering Heights, under Heathcliff's influence, she annoyed Hindley, laughed at Joseph, and was rude to me. But at Thrushcross Grange, which she often visited, she showed a different, calmer side of her character, and was polite, intelligent and amusing. The Lintons all liked her, and poor Edgar had fallen in love with her.

Heathcliff was sixteen at this time. He did not have time to study any more, and the long hours of work on the farm made him tired and dull. There was always an angry expression on his face, and he did not even try to keep himself clean and tidy. He seemed to *want* people to dislike him. Catherine and he still spent time together, when he was not working in the fields, but he no longer expressed his fondness for her in words, and he looked angry if she touched or kissed him.

One afternoon, when Hindley had gone into town, Heathcliff came into the main room after lunch. I was helping Catherine to arrange her hair, as she had invited Edgar Linton to visit her while Hindley was absent.

'Catherine, are you going anywhere this afternoon?' asked Heathcliff. 'Why have you got that silk dress on? Nobody's visiting you, I hope.'

'No-o, I don't think so,' replied Catherine, looking quickly at me. 'But you should be at work by now, Heathcliff.'

'That devil Hindley isn't away very often. I'm taking a holiday. I won't work any more today. I'm staying with you this afternoon. He'll never know.'

Catherine thought for a moment. Somehow she had to prepare him for Edgar's visit. 'Isabella and Edgar said they might call here this afternoon. If they come, you'll be scolded for not working.'

'Tell Ellen to say you're busy and can't see them,' he said. 'Those friends of yours take up all your time. You spend most of your evenings with them, not with me.'

'Well, why should I always spend my time with you?' she asked crossly. 'What can you talk about? How can you amuse me?'

'You never told me before that you didn't like my company, Catherine!' cried Heathcliff.

Just then we heard a horse outside, and there was a light knock on the door. Edgar Linton entered, his handsome face full of delight at receiving Catherine's unexpected invitation. I wondered if Catherine was comparing her two friends, as Edgar came in and Heathcliff ran out.

'I haven't come too soon, have I?' asked Edgar politely.

'No,' answered Catherine. 'Leave us alone, Ellen.'

'I'm just doing my work, miss,' I replied, pretending to dust the furniture. Hindley had told me to be present if Edgar Linton came to visit Catherine.

She came up to me, and whispered crossly, 'Go away, Ellen!' Keeping her back to Edgar, she cruelly scratched my arm.

'Oh!' I screamed, to show Edgar what had happened. 'What a wicked thing to do, miss! You have no right to hurt me!'

'I didn't touch you, you lying creature!' she cried angrily, and, unable to control herself, hit me hard on the face.

'Catherine, love! Catherine!' cried Edgar, shocked.

The baby, Hareton, who followed me everywhere, immediately started sobbing and saying, 'Wicked aunt Catherine!'

She picked him up and shook the poor child until he screamed. Edgar rushed up to her and tried to stop her. At once she turned and hit him over the ear as hard as she could.

The young man looked very pale and went straight to the door.

'Where are you going, Edgar Linton?' she asked. 'Don't leave me! I shall be miserable all night!'

'Can I stay after you have hit me?' he replied. 'You've made me afraid and ashamed of you. I won't come here again!'

'Well, go then, if you want to!' she cried. 'I'm going to cry until I'm ill!' and she dropped on to the floor, her shoulders shaking and the tears rolling down her face.

Edgar managed to get as far as the door. But here he hesitated, and I called out to him to encourage him to leave.

'Miss is just a selfish child, sir! You'd better ride home and forget her!'

But as he could not stop looking at her, I knew there was no hope for him. Nothing would keep him away from her now. And sure enough, he came back into the room and shut the door. This time I left them alone, and stayed in the kitchen with little Hareton, but when I came to warn them that Hindley had returned, I realized that their quarrel had only brought them closer together.

CHAPTER 6

Heathcliff disappears

———— HINDLEY CAME INTO the kitchen, swearing terribly,
1778–9 just as I was about to hide little Hareton in a cupboard.
———— I was always afraid that Hindley would hurt his small
son, either by accident or on purpose, when he was drunk, so I
tried to keep Hareton out of the way. But this time Hindley
discovered my plan.

'Ah, you keep my son in a cupboard, do you!' he cried angrily,
picking up a sharp kitchen knife. 'With the devil's help I'll make
you swallow this, Ellen!' And he pushed the knife between my
teeth.

I was never afraid he would hurt *me*, and calmly took the
knife out of my mouth.

'But that can't be my son, can it?' he continued aggressively,
staring at the frightened little boy. 'If it is, he should be punished
for not running to greet his father. Perhaps I'll cut his ears off!'
And then suddenly his manner changed. 'No, Hareton, darling,
don't cry! Kiss me, kiss your father! What? You won't? Then I'll
break your neck!'

Poor Hareton, screaming wildly, was carried upstairs by his
father. Suddenly Hindley stopped on the stairs to listen, almost
forgetting what he was holding. Heathcliff had come into the
house and stood at the bottom of the stairs, looking up. Just
then the child jumped out of Hindley's arms and fell. I only had
time to gasp in horror, before I saw that Heathcliff had caught
him.

Heathcliff stared down at the child he was holding. He must

23

Just then the child jumped out of Hindley's arms and fell.

have felt sorry he had saved the life of his enemy's son. I rushed
to take the poor little boy in my arms, and Hindley came slowly
downstairs.

'Look what you've done, Mr Hindley!' I cried. 'You nearly
killed your own son! What would his mother say if she were
alive?'

'Take him away, Ellen. And you, Heathcliff, go away too. I
won't murder you tonight, unless perhaps I set the house on fire.

24

But that depends how I feel.' And he poured himself a drink.

'Don't drink any more, Mr Hindley!' I begged.

'What difference does it make?' he growled. 'Get out, both of you! To the devil with you!'

We left him swearing at us, and went back into the kitchen.

'It's a pity he can't kill himself with drink,' muttered Heathcliff. 'Dr Kenneth says he'll live longer than any of us, he's so strong.'

He walked out of the door and, I thought, into the fields. In fact I discovered later that he was sitting just under the window, and could hear everything that was said in the kitchen.

I was singing little Hareton to sleep when Catherine came in.

'Are you alone, Ellen?' she whispered. 'Where's Heathcliff?'

'He's out on the farm,' I answered.

She looked sad and worried, and I even saw a tear or two on her face. But I had not forgotten how she had lied, and behaved so badly to me as well as to Edgar Linton, so I did not feel sorry for her, or encourage her to talk.

'Ellen, will you keep a secret for me?' she asked in the end, giving me her sweetest smile. 'I must tell you! I need your advice. Today Edgar Linton has asked me to marry him, and I gave him an answer. Now, before I tell you if it was yes or no, you tell me which I should have said.'

'Really, Miss Catherine, how can I know? Perhaps you should have refused him. He must be a fool to ask you, after you were so rude and violent this afternoon.'

'Well, I accepted him, Ellen!' she said crossly. 'But should I have done so? Should I? What do you think?'

'First, do you love him?' I asked.

'Of course I do,' she replied.

'Why do you love him, Miss Catherine?'

'Well, I do, that's enough. Well, because he's handsome, and a pleasant companion.'

'Oh, that's bad,' I said, shaking my head.

'And because he loves me.'

'That's worse.'

'And because he'll be rich, and I shall be the most important woman for miles around.'

'Worst of all. But there are several other handsome, rich young men in the world. Why don't you marry one of them?'

'I don't know any of them. I only know Edgar.'

'Well, I don't know why you're unhappy, Miss Catherine. Your brother will be pleased, and Mr Edgar's parents will, too. You love Edgar, and Edgar loves you. What's the problem?'

'*Here!* And *here!*' replied Catherine, beating her head and her chest. 'In my heart and soul I know I'm wrong! Ellen, I can't live apart from Heathcliff! He is more myself than I am. Our souls are the same! I have nothing in common with Edgar. But I can't marry Heathcliff now! Hindley has made him become a poor, dull farm worker. He'll never know how I love him.'

I suddenly heard a movement outside the window, and saw Heathcliff stand up and walk away. I realized he had been listening until he heard Catherine say she could not marry him. Then he stayed to hear no more.

'Quiet, Miss Catherine!' I said. 'Just imagine how hard it will be for Heathcliff when you marry Mr Edgar! He'll have no friends at all when you leave him.'

'Leave him? Why should we be separated?' she asked angrily. 'Who will separate us? Nobody will dare! Edgar must learn to accept him as my friend. Didn't you ever think, Ellen, that if Heathcliff and I married, we would be very poor? But if I marry Edgar, I can help Heathcliff with my husband's money.'

'That's the worst reason you've given so far for marrying Mr Edgar,' I replied, shocked.

'It isn't! Heathcliff is more important to me than myself. My love for Edgar is like the leaves on the trees – I'm sure time will change it. But my love for Heathcliff is like the rocks in the ground – not beautiful, but necessary and unchanging. He's always, always in my heart — '

Just then Joseph entered the kitchen. I whispered to Catherine that I was sure Heathcliff had heard some of what she said. She jumped up, frightened, and rushed outside. But although we all looked everywhere for Heathcliff, there was no sign of him that night, or for many nights in the future.

At about midnight, while we were still waiting for him to come home, we noticed the wind was getting stronger. We could hear it whistling down the chimney, and howling all around the house. Suddenly there was a terrible crash of thunder, and the branch of a tree fell on to the roof. We were not hurt, but Joseph immediately dropped on to his knees to pray. The rain was beating down on the windows, but Catherine stayed outside, although by now her hair and clothes were completely wet.

In the end we all went to bed. I managed to persuade Catherine to come in, but she insisted on sleeping in the kitchen, in case Heathcliff returned during the night. In the morning we discovered that she had caught a fever, as a result of getting wet. She became seriously ill, and it was several weeks before Dr Kenneth would allow her out of bed.

When she recovered, she was invited to stay for a while at Thrushcross Grange. Unfortunately old Mr and Mrs Linton caught the fever too, and died within a few days of each other. Catherine returned to us, prouder and quicker-tempered than ever, but not as strong as before.

'If she gets ill again, it could be fatal,' Dr Kenneth warned us. 'My advice to you is to do whatever she wants, and don't make her angry!' So we had to obey all her orders, and Joseph and I were not allowed to scold her any more.

Edgar Linton was still in love with her, and thought himself the happiest man on earth when he married her three years after his parents' death. She insisted on having me with her, so we moved together to Thrushcross Grange, although I was very sad to leave little Hareton with his father.

It's very late, Mr Lockwood. I think you should go to bed, or you'll be ill tomorrow. I can tell you the rest of the story another time.

Four weeks later In fact I *was* ill the next day, and have been ill since then. The terrible night I spent at Wuthering Heights was the cause of my illness, and I blame Mr Heathcliff for it. Dr Kenneth has warned me I won't be able to go out until the spring. All I can do is lie in bed, listening to the howling wind and staring at the grey northern sky.

So I've decided to ask Mrs Dean to come upstairs and finish telling me her story. She tells me she's happy to continue.

CHAPTER 7

Heathcliff returns

——— WELL, SIR, WHEN Miss Catherine became Mrs
1783 Linton, and we went to live at Thrushcross Grange, I
——— must say I was surprised and pleased by her behaviour.
She showed great fondness for her husband, and for his sister,
Isabella. He, of course, was very anxious that no one should
disobey her, or make her angry. If she was depressed for a time,
he blamed it on the illness she had had, and was sympathetic.
But for most of the time, I believe they shared a deep and
growing love for each other.

Unfortunately this happiness did not last. One evening I was
bringing in a basket of apples from the garden, when a voice
behind me said, 'Ellen, is that you?'

It was a deep, rather unusual voice. I turned, to see a tall, dark
man in the shadow near the kitchen door.

'Don't you know me?' he asked. 'Look, I'm not a stranger!'

'What!' I cried in surprise, for it had been four years since he
disappeared. 'Heathcliff! Is it really you?'

'Yes,' he replied, looking up at the windows of the house. 'Are
they at home? Where is she? Tell me, Ellen! I must speak to her!'

'I'm not sure if you should see her,' I hesitated. 'Will the shock
be too much for her?'

'Go and tell her I'm here, Ellen!' he said impatiently. 'Don't
make me suffer like this!'

I left him at the door, and went upstairs to find Mr and Mrs
Linton. They were sitting quietly together, looking out over the
peaceful valley. The room, and the view, and the two people,

seemed so calm that I did not want to disturb them. But I had to deliver my message.

'A man wants to see you, madam,' I muttered.

'I'll go downstairs and see him then,' replied Catherine. 'Bring the tea up, Ellen, while I'm away.' She left the room.

'Who is it, Ellen?' asked Mr Edgar.

'It's that Heathcliff, sir. You remember, he used to live at Wuthering Heights.'

'What! The gipsy, who worked on the farm?' he cried.

'Mrs Linton would be angry if she heard you talking about him like that, sir. She was very upset when he ran away. She's very fond of him, you know.'

Mr Edgar put his head out of the window and called to his wife, 'Don't stand there in the cold, love! Bring the person in, if it's anyone special.'

Catherine rushed upstairs and into the room, wild and breathless. She threw her arms round her husband's neck.

'Oh Edgar darling! Heathcliff's come back!'

'Well, well,' said Mr Edgar crossly, 'there's no need to get excited.'

'I know you didn't like him,' she said, 'but please, I beg you to be friends with him now. Shall I ask him to come up?'

'You're suggesting inviting him up here, into our sitting-room? Don't you think the kitchen is more suitable for him?'

Catherine looked at her husband, half angry and half laughing. 'No,' she said, 'I can't sit in the kitchen. Ellen, bring two tables, one for your master and Miss Isabella, the other for Heathcliff and myself. We'll sit apart from them, as we're of a lower class! Will that please you, Edgar darling? Decide quickly! I must have him near me!'

'Ellen, *you* go and bring him up,' said Mr Edgar. 'And

Catherine, try not to behave foolishly. Remember, he's only a servant!'

When Heathcliff entered the sitting-room, I was surprised to see how much he had changed. He wore a confident, intelligent expression on his face, and his manner was no longer rough. Although I recognized the same black fire in his eyes, the farm boy had become a gentleman.

Mr Edgar was as surprised as I was, but welcomed Heathcliff as politely as he could. However, he grew more and more annoyed as he watched his wife's delighted face. She could not take her eyes off Heathcliff.

'Tomorrow I won't be able to believe that I've seen and touched you, Heathcliff!' she cried, catching hold of his hands. 'But how cruel of you to run away and keep silent for four years, and never think of me!'

'I've thought of you more than you've thought of me,' he replied quietly. 'I heard you had married, Catherine, and I came, just to see you once, and then take my revenge on your brother Hindley. Your welcome may change my plans. You know, I've had a bitter, hard life since I last heard your voice, and if I've survived, it's all because of you!'

'Catherine,' said Mr Edgar, trying to remain polite, 'please pour out the tea, or it will be cold. Mr Heathcliff will have a long walk to wherever he's staying tonight, and I'm thirsty.'

But Catherine was too excited, and Mr Edgar too angry, to drink any tea. After a while their guest left. We discovered that he had been invited to stay at Wuthering Heights, by Hindley. I could not understand why Hindley, who hated him, would want his company, and I felt sure it would have been better for all of us if Heathcliff had never come back.

Catherine could not keep her happiness to herself. In the

middle of the night she woke me to talk about Heathcliff.

'I just can't sleep, Ellen!' she said. 'And Edgar won't listen when I tell him how happy I am! He's so selfish!'

'He never liked Heathcliff,' I replied, 'and he'll be angry if you go on talking about him. You think he's weak, but he could be as determined as you, about something he thinks is important.'

'No!' she laughed. 'I have such confidence in Edgar's love that I think I could *kill* him, and he wouldn't blame me for it. He will have to learn to accept Heathcliff as my friend.'

'Do you know why Heathcliff is staying at Wuthering Heights?'

'Oh, yes. He explained that he went there to look for me. Hindley asked him to play cards, and when he discovered Heathcliff had a lot of money, invited him to stay there. You know how greedy my brother is. He'll make Heathcliff pay rent, *and* hope to win money from him at cards. Heathcliff wants to stay there to be near me. I'm so happy, Ellen! And I want everyone around me to be happy too!'

Catherine behaved so sweetly to her husband in the next few days that Thrushcross Grange seemed full of sunshine, and in spite of his doubts, Mr Edgar allowed Heathcliff to visit her regularly. However, Heathcliff's visits produced a result which none of us had expected. Isabella, Mr Edgar's sister, a pretty girl of eighteen, suddenly declared that she was in love with Heathcliff. Mr Edgar, who loved her dearly, was shocked. He knew that if he and Catherine had no sons, Isabella would inherit the considerable Linton fortune. He did not like the idea of the fortune passing to Heathcliff, as Isabella's husband. But more importantly, he suspected that Heathcliff was hiding his true wickedness under his gentlemanly appearance.

Catherine tried hard to persuade Isabella that Heathcliff was not worth loving, but poor Isabella was jealous of Catherine's relationship with Heathcliff and would not listen. Finally, Catherine told Heathcliff himself that Isabella was in love with him. She thought she knew what his answer would be.

'How could I ever love that stupid girl?' he asked. 'She has a miserable pale face, and weak blue eyes, just like your husband! But . . . she will inherit the family wealth from him, won't she?'

'That's true,' replied Catherine. 'But don't think about that, Heathcliff. I hope Edgar and I will have several sons, and then *they* will inherit it.'

Catherine did not speak of this matter again, but I am sure Heathcliff often thought about it. I watched him carefully in the next few days. I hoped he would do nothing to hurt Mr Edgar, who was a kind master to me. I was worried, too, about what was happening at Wuthering Heights. Hindley and his son Hareton seemed like lost sheep to me, and I knew there was a wicked wolf just waiting for the chance to attack them.

CHAPTER 8

Catherine is ill

——— THE NEXT TIME Heathcliff came to Thrushcross
1783 Grange, he met Isabella by chance in front of the
——— house. I was watching from the kitchen window, as he
went up to her, and, supposing that no one else could see him,
kissed her.

'Look, madam!' I cried to Catherine, who was passing
through the kitchen. 'That devil Heathcliff told you he could
never love Miss Isabella! And now he's kissing her!'

So when Heathcliff entered the house, Catherine was ready to
scold him.

'Leave Isabella alone, Heathcliff!' she ordered. 'You'll make
Edgar angry!'

'You think I'm afraid of that weak little creature?' he
growled. 'Anyway, what difference does it make to you? I can
kiss her if she likes it. I'm not *your* husband, you needn't be
jealous of *me*!'

'I'm not jealous of you!' replied Catherine. 'If you like
Isabella, you can marry her. But *do* you like her?'

'It's *you* I want to talk about, Catherine. You know you've
treated me badly. And I'm going to have my revenge! Thank you
for telling me Isabella's secret. I swear I'll make good use
of it!'

At this point I went to look for my master, and told him that
Catherine and Heathcliff were quarrelling in the kitchen.

'How can my wife call that man a friend?' he cried angrily.
'I've been too weak with her. I can't allow him to visit her any

34

more. Call two servants, Ellen.' He went to the kitchen. I followed him, telling the servants to wait in the hall.

'Catherine!' said Mr Edgar to his wife as he entered. 'Do you think it's right to listen to this wicked man's talk?'

'Have you been listening at the door, Edgar?' asked Catherine coldly. Heathcliff laughed, which made Mr Edgar even angrier.

'You, sir,' he said to Heathcliff, 'are poisoning our family life. I should never have accepted you as Catherine's friend. I must inform you that you will never be allowed to enter this house again, and that if you don't leave within three minutes, you will be thrown out.'

'Well, well!' replied Heathcliff, looking scornfully at Mr Edgar's small figure. 'So, you're going to throw me out yourself, are you?'

My master looked towards the door. I realized he wanted to call the servants, as he knew he was not strong enough to fight Heathcliff alone. But Catherine must have guessed his plan. She hurried to the door and locked it. Mr Edgar looked at her in angry surprise.

'You must fight him like a gentleman, without anyone to help you!' she told her husband. 'That'll teach you to scold me!'

Mr Edgar tried to get hold of the key, but she threw it quickly into the hottest part of the fire. He went very pale, and could not stop his whole body trembling.

'Oh Edgar!' cried his wife. 'You've lost the fight already! You aren't a man, you're a mouse!'

'So that,' said Heathcliff, pointing at Mr Edgar, 'is the thing you preferred to me, Catherine. Is he crying, or is he going to die of fear?'

He went up to look more closely at Mr Edgar, who suddenly recovered and hit Heathcliff hard on the neck. While Heathcliff

'So, you're going to throw me out yourself, are you?'

was getting his breath back, Mr Edgar walked out of the other kitchen door into the garden.

'Now you'll never be able to come here again,' said Catherine to Heathcliff. 'Go away quickly! He'll return with men and guns.'

Heathcliff was sensible enough to take her advice. He broke down the locked door and escaped, just as the master and his men returned.

Catherine, who was over-excited, ordered me to go upstairs with her. I hoped she would not discover that I had told Mr Edgar about her quarrel with Heathcliff.

'I'm wild with anger, Ellen!' she said, when we reached the sitting-room. 'All this trouble is because of Isabella! Tell Edgar I'm in danger of becoming seriously ill. I hope it's true, I want to frighten him. He's upset me badly. Why did he listen to us talking in the kitchen? Heathcliff says wicked things, but I know I can control him. Well, if I can't have Heathcliff as my friend, if Edgar is going to be mean and jealous, I'll try to break both their hearts by breaking my own. You must remind Edgar how quick-tempered I am, and what Dr Kenneth said about my health. Edgar must let me do what I want!'

I did not feel sympathetic towards Catherine, and certainly did not want to frighten my poor master by telling him she was ill. As I was leaving the room, however, he entered.

'Catherine,' he said, 'you must tell me one thing. You must choose between me and Heathcliff. Which do you intend to have?'

'Leave me alone!' she cried wildly. 'I'm ill, can't you see, I can't even stand! Edgar, leave me!'

She fell, stiff and pale, on to the floor. Mr Edgar looked very frightened.

'Don't worry, sir,' I whispered to him. 'She told me she would try to make you afraid by pretending to be ill.'

Unfortunately she heard me. She jumped up, her hair loose and her eyes staring, and rushed to her bedroom. We heard the key turn in the lock.

For the next few days she refused to speak to anyone, even me. I took her food up to her room, but she would not eat. Mr Edgar spent his time in the library, and did not ask about his wife. He hoped, I suppose, that she would come and ask him to forgive her. But I knew she was too proud to do that.

On the third day she unlocked her door and called me. She ate and drank eagerly, then lay down again.

'Oh, why don't I die, since no one cares about me!' she muttered. 'Edgar doesn't love me at all! What is he doing all this time, Ellen?'

'He's reading books in the library, madam,' I answered.

'Reading books!' she cried, shocked. 'And I'm dying up here! My God! Does he know how I've changed, how ill I am? Can't you tell him I'm seriously ill, Ellen?'

'You forget, Mrs Linton, that you've eaten tonight. I'm sure you'll feel better tomorrow morning.' I still wanted to make her realize how selfish she was being, although I was a little worried by her pale, almost ghostly face.

'I begin to see that you don't like me, Ellen. How strange! I always thought everybody loved me! Now they are all my enemies – Isabella and Edgar and you! I'll die with cold faces around me! I've had terrible dreams these past few nights, you know. Open the window, Ellen! I'm so hot!'

I refused, as it was the middle of winter. She was feverish.

'Who is that over there?' she asked, staring at her own face in a mirror opposite her bed. I could not make her understand it was herself, and I began to be afraid that her illness was real.

'Stay with me, Ellen,' she cried, holding my hand. 'I'm

frightened of that face! I'm frightened of being alone! I wish I were in my bed at Wuthering Heights, with the wind howling through the trees. Do let me feel a breath of air from the moors, just one breath!'

I opened the window for a moment, then closed it. The cold air seemed to calm her. 'I wish I were a young girl again, wild and free, out on the moors with Heathcliff! Open the window again, wider this time! Why won't you?'

'Because I don't want you to die of cold,' I replied.

'But it's my only chance of life!' she cried, jumping out of bed and going to the window. I tried to force her back to bed, but her fever made her surprisingly strong. We looked out together into the icy darkness. There was no moon, and no lights were visible anywhere. But Catherine was sure she could see Wuthering Heights.

'Look!' she said. 'There's my old home, and the churchyard near it. I won't lie there alone, Heathcliff! I won't rest until you're in the grave with me!'

I was still holding her back from the window, and wondering what to do next, when Mr Edgar entered.

'Please help, sir,' I called, 'Mrs Linton is ill.'

'Catherine's ill?' he gasped. 'Shut the window, Ellen! Catherine! Why — '

When he saw his wife's face, he was so shocked that he stopped speaking and stared at her in horror. She was almost unconscious and did not recognize him at first.

'Ah, it's you, is it, Edgar Linton?' she said after a few moments. 'You don't come when you're wanted, and now you come when you're not wanted! But whatever you say, nothing can keep me from my home, my place of rest, out there in the open air, with a gravestone at my head!'

'She's feverish, sir, and doesn't know what she's saying,' I whispered. 'If she has food and rest, she'll recover.'

'I want no further advice from you, Ellen Dean,' said Mr Edgar coldly. 'You knew how ill she was, and you didn't tell me!'

I ran downstairs and out of the kitchen door to fetch the doctor. I thought I heard the sound of horses in the distance, which seemed strange at two o'clock in the morning. And when I found Dr Kenneth, he told me someone had seen Isabella and Heathcliff meeting secretly in the garden earlier that evening.

That night none of us slept. We all sat together and waited, while the doctor stayed with his patient. He told us he hoped that Catherine would recover, if we kept her very quiet.

In the morning we discovered that Isabella's room was empty. She had run away with Heathcliff! When Mr Edgar heard the news, he just said, 'She chose to go with him. Don't speak to me of her again. I no longer think of her as my sister.'

CHAPTER 9

Isabella's story

FOR TWO MONTHS we heard nothing of Isabella
1784   or Heathcliff. During that time Catherine was
        dangerously ill with brain fever, and Dr Kenneth
warned us that even if she recovered, her brain would never return to normal. However she did seem to get better, and no one could have been happier than my master, when he saw her sitting up in bed for the first time, and beginning to take an

interest in the people and things around her. He loved her so much, and took such good care of her, that I really thought she would recover. There was another reason for her to live. She was expecting a baby, and we all hoped she would have a son, who would inherit the Linton fortune.

Then Mr Edgar received a letter from Isabella, telling him that she and Heathcliff were married. With it was a long letter for me, which said:

Wuthering Heights

Dear Ellen,

I arrived here last night and heard that Catherine is ill. My brother refuses to write to me, so you are the only one I can write to. Tell Edgar I still love him and Catherine, and want to return to Thrushcross Grange, but I can't!

The rest of this letter is for you alone, Ellen. Two questions – how did you manage to get on with the people in this house? They don't seem human! And (this interests me very much) what is Mr Heathcliff? A man? A madman? A devil? When you come to visit me, you must explain to me what sort of creature I've married. And you must come very soon, with a message from Edgar.

Heathcliff brought me here last night. This house is going to be my home, he says. He disappeared as soon as we arrived, so I entered the kitchen alone. What a miserable, depressing place it is now, Ellen! By the fire stood a dirty child. I realized he must be Catherine's nephew, Hareton, and tried to shake his hand. But he greeted me by swearing at me, so I went into the hall to find somebody else. When I knocked at another door, it was opened by a tall, thin man, with long, dirty hair hanging down to his shoulders. I knew this must be Hindley Earnshaw, Catherine's brother and Hareton's father. His eyes, and Hareton's, reminded me of Catherine.

'What do you want?' he asked roughly.

'My name was Isabella Linton,' I replied. 'Now I'm married to Mr Heathcliff.'

'Ah, so that devil has returned! Good!' he growled.

You can imagine, Ellen, how unhappy I felt in that unpleasant house. I knew that only four miles away was my real home, Thrushcross Grange, containing the only people I loved in the world. But those four miles were like an ocean, which I could not cross! Don't tell Edgar or Catherine this, but I had hoped to find a friend at Wuthering Heights, someone to support me against Heathcliff. Now I realized that no one here would help me.

After a long silence I said, 'Please ask a maid to show me my bedroom. I'm tired after my journey.'

'We have no maids here,' he answered. 'Joseph will show you Heathcliff's room, if you like. And – and – you'd better lock the bedroom door tonight!'

'Why, Mr Earnshaw?' I asked. I did not want to lock myself in with Heathcliff.

He brought out a gun, which had a knife attached to it.

'Look at this,' he said. 'Every night I try to open his bedroom door. Up to now he's locked it. But one night he'll forget, and then I'll kill him!'

'Why do you hate him so much?' I asked.

'Because he's taken everything from me!' he shouted angrily. 'There's nothing left for Hareton to inherit! But I'm going to get it all back! and *his* money too, and then his blood. Then the devil can have his soul!'

He seemed mad to me, Ellen. I left him, and went to find the old servant, Joseph. It seemed that Heathcliff's room was locked, and there were no guest bedrooms, so in the end I slept on a chair in the child's room. What a welcome to my new home!

I know Heathcliff blames Edgar for Catherine's illness. He has warned me he'll make *me* suffer for it. Oh, I do hate him – I'm so miserable – I've been such a fool! Don't tell anyone at Thrushcross Grange about this, Ellen. Come quickly – don't disappoint me!

Isabella

As soon as I had read this, I asked Mr Edgar if I could take a message from him to his sister.

'You may visit her this afternoon, Ellen, if you like. Tell her I'm not angry, just sorry to have lost her. I can't imagine she will ever be happy. I shall never visit her or write to her.'

When I arrived at Wuthering Heights that afternoon, I was shocked to see how much worse the house looked than when I used to live there. I realized that Hindley did not care what conditions he lived in, and Joseph clearly spent more time praying than cleaning. Heathcliff and Isabella were both in the main room. Heathcliff looked more like a gentleman than I had ever seen him, but his wife had not bothered to brush her hair or change her dress. I had to explain to poor Isabella that Mr Edgar had refused to write to her. She cried a little when she heard that. Then Heathcliff asked me question after question about Catherine's illness.

'If you really love her,' I told him, 'you'll keep away from her now. She mustn't be over-excited. Her health will always be weak. And her loving husband is a very good nurse to her!'

'Her loving husband!' repeated Heathcliff scornfully. 'Don't compare my feeling for her with his! No, Ellen, before you leave this house, I'll make you promise to arrange a meeting for me with Catherine. I *must* see her!'

'I'll never agree to that,' I said. 'She's just beginning to recover. She's almost forgotten you, and now you want to upset her again!'

'Ellen, you know as well as I do that she can never forget me! If she thinks once of Edgar Linton, she thinks a thousand times of me! He can't love her as I can! And Catherine has a heart as deep as mine!'

'Catherine and Edgar are very fond of each other!' said Isabella suddenly. 'Don't speak of my brother like that!'

'Your dear brother doesn't care enough about you to write to you,' replied Heathcliff, smiling sourly.

'That's because he doesn't know how much I've suffered,' she answered quietly, turning away to hide the tears on her face.

'Sir,' I said, 'it seems to me that Miss Isabella, Mrs Heathcliff, I should say, is unhappy. You must treat her kindly. Try to look after her. Let her have a maid, for example.'

'I'm not going to be soft with her,' he replied with a laugh. 'She was stupid enough to run away with me. I never pretended to love her. Now I think she's beginning to realize that I scorn her. She's an even weaker fool than her brother, but she's going to be useful to me. That's why I'm keeping her with me.'

'Ellen, he says he married me to have his revenge on Edgar! But I won't let him carry out his plan, whatever it is! I'll die, or I'll see him dead first!'

'You're getting violent, Isabella!' said Heathcliff. 'Go upstairs now. I want to speak to Ellen Dean in private. Go on!' And he pushed her roughly out of the door.

'Don't you feel pity for her?' I asked, when we were alone. 'Have you ever felt pity for anybody in your life?'

'Why should I? She's just like an insect under my foot. The more she cries, the more I enjoy hurting her. Now, Ellen, listen. I'll wait every day and every evening in the Grange garden, until I find a chance to see Catherine. If I meet Edgar Linton or his servants, I'll shoot them. But don't you think it'd be better to avoid a fight? You could tell me when she'll be alone. Then there'll be no violence.'

I argued and complained, and refused fifty times, but in the end he forced me to agree. I promised to let him know when Edgar Linton was away from home. I suppose it was wrong of me, but I hoped it would be Heathcliff's last meeting with Catherine.

CHAPTER 10

Heathcliff visits Catherine for the last time

1784

HEATHCLIFF HAD GIVEN me a letter for Catherine, but I decided not to show it to her until Mr Edgar was out of the house. My chance came four days after my visit to Wuthering Heights. As it was a Sunday, Mr Edgar and all the servants went to church, leaving me alone to look after Catherine.

She was sitting downstairs, by an open window, enjoying the spring sunshine. Her appearance had changed since her illness, but there was a strange beauty in her pale face. She did not read or sew any more, but used to sit there silently, staring into the distance. Her eyes seemed fixed on something far away, something beyond normal sight.

I showed her the letter, but she looked confused and could not seem to understand it, so I had to explain.

'It's from Mr Heathcliff,' I said gently. 'He's in the garden, and wants to see you. What shall I tell him?'

She said nothing, but bent forward in her chair to listen. We both heard someone coming through the hall. Heathcliff had realized the house was almost empty, and had found an open door. Catherine looked eagerly towards the entrance to the room. He appeared, and in two steps was by her side. For five whole minutes he held her in his arms and kissed her again and again. It gave him great pain to look at her face. He could see, as I could, that she would never recover, that she was certain to die.

'Oh, Catherine! Oh, my life! How can I bear it!' he cried.

'You and Edgar have broken my heart,' said Catherine. 'And you both want *me* to pity *you*! How strong you are, Heathcliff! You'll live for years after my death! Will you forget me, and be happy with others, when I'm in my grave?'

'It's wicked of you to say that, Catherine. You know your words will burn for ever in my memory after you've left me. You know I could never forget you!'

'I don't want you to suffer more than I do, Heathcliff. I only want us to be together, always.'

Heathcliff turned away, his shoulders shaking.

'That isn't *my* Heathcliff,' Catherine said to me. 'I'll always love *my* Heathcliff, and take him with me. He's in my soul, you see. Oh, Ellen, I do want to escape from this prison. There's a beautiful world waiting for me out there. You feel sorry for me now because I'm ill. Well, very soon *I'll* feel sorry for *you*, because I'll be beyond you all!'

Heathcliff turned towards her, his fierce eyes wet. For a moment they looked at each other, and then they were in each other's arms again. No one could have separated them.

'How cruel you've been to me, Catherine!' he cried wildly. 'You loved me, so why did you marry Edgar Linton? It's all your fault! *I* haven't broken your heart, *you've* broken it! And you've broken mine too! Do you think I *want* to live after you are dead?'

'If I've done wrong, I'm dying for it!' sobbed Catherine. 'It's your fault too, Heathcliff! You left me, remember? But I forgive you. Now forgive me!'

'It's hard to forgive, when I look at your sad eyes, and feel your thin hands. Kiss me again, Catherine! I forgive you for making me suffer, but how can I forgive you for dying?'

Catherine sobbed quietly, hiding her face in his shoulder, and tears rolled down Heathcliff's dark face.

Suddenly I noticed, through the window, the servants coming back from church. I was afraid Mr Edgar would find Heathcliff with Catherine.

'My master will be here in a moment,' I warned them.

'I must go, Catherine,' said Heathcliff.

'No, no!' she screamed. 'Don't go! It's the last time! Edgar won't hurt us! Heathcliff, I'll die if you go!'

'All right, my darling, I'll stay. If he shot me in your arms, I'd die happy.'

At that moment my master appeared at the door. When he saw Heathcliff holding his wife, he went pale with anger.

'Here, take care of her first,' said Heathcliff, putting Catherine in her husband's arms, 'then speak to me later if you wish.' He walked out of the house.

Catherine seemed to be unconscious, and Mr Edgar was so

worried about her that he forgot about Heathcliff for the moment. She recovered a little, but did not recognize any of us, and was clearly very ill. We put her to bed immediately, and at twelve o'clock that night her daughter, Cathy, was born, two months early. That's the young lady you saw at Wuthering Heights, Mr Lockwood. Two hours later, Catherine died, without calling for Heathcliff, or recognizing Edgar. My poor master was in the depths of despair. I thought it was very unfortunate that Catherine had only given him a daughter, not a son. Now the Linton fortune would pass to Isabella and her husband after Mr Edgar's death.

Catherine's dead body lay peacefully on her bed. In death she looked more beautiful than in life. I wondered if she was now 'beyond us all', as she had said, and hoped that her soul had found a home with God.

In the morning I went to look for Heathcliff. I found him in the Grange garden, where he had been waiting for news all night.

'She's dead, I know!' he called to me as I came closer. 'Don't cry, she doesn't need your tears! Tell me – tell me, how did – ?' He tried to say her name, but could not manage it. 'How did she die?' he said at last, staring fiercely at me. 'Don't be sorry for me, I don't want your pity!'

'Poor creature!' I thought. 'You have a heart just like other men, but you are too proud to show it!'

Aloud I said, 'She died quietly, in her sleep. Her life finished in a gentle dream. I hope she wakes as calmly in the other world!'

'Where are you, Catherine?' he cried in despair. 'Don't leave me here, where I can't find you! I pray that you will never rest while I'm alive. You said I killed you – haunt me then! Murdered people do haunt their murderers, I believe. Come back as a ghost – drive me mad – I don't care! Oh, God! I can't bear it! I cannot live without you, my soul!'

He howled like a wild animal, and hit his forehead several times against a tree, until the wood was covered in blood. I knew I could no longer help him, so I left him.

Catherine was buried the following Friday. Her brother Hindley, although invited, did not come, and Isabella was not invited, so it was only Mr Edgar and the servants who attended the ceremony. To our surprise, she was not buried in the church with the Lintons, nor with the Earnshaws. She lies in an open corner of the churchyard, where she can breathe the air from the moors. Her husband's grave is next to hers.

He howled like a wild animal.

49

CHAPTER 11

Isabella escapes

—————— THAT FRIDAY EVENING the wind changed, and
1784 brought first rain, then snow. Next morning the spring
—————— flowers were all hidden under deep snow. Mr Edgar
stayed in his room. I was in the sitting-room with the baby,
when I was surprised to hear a girl's voice behind me. I turned
round, and saw it was Isabella Heathcliff. I was quite shocked
by her appearance. Her hair was loose, and wet with snow and
rain. She wore a light silk dress and thin shoes, which did not
seem at all suitable for a long walk in the snow. Under her ear
was a deep wound, which was bleeding. Her face was scratched
and bruised, and she looked very tired. I could see that she was
expecting a baby.

'I've run all the way here from Wuthering Heights,' she said,
gasping for breath. 'I couldn't count how many times I've fallen
down! Ellen, please ask a maid to find some dry clothes for me,
and then I'll go on to the village. I'm not staying here.'

'First, my dear young lady,' I told her, 'you'll get warm and
dry, and I'll put a bandage on that wound. Then we'll have some
tea.' She was so exhausted that she let me help her without
protesting, and finally we sat down together near the fire with
our cups of tea.

'Oh, Ellen,' she said, 'I cried bitterly when I heard of
Catherine's death, you know. And Heathcliff is desperately sad!
But I can't feel sorry for him. This is the last thing of his I've
got,' and she took off her gold wedding-ring and threw it in the
fire. 'I'll never go back to him. But I can't stay here, in case he

50

'I've run all the way here from Wuthering Heights.'

comes to find me. And anyway I don't want to beg for Edgar's help, or make trouble for him. To escape from Heathcliff I must go a long way away. How could Catherine have liked him, Ellen? I wish he would die, and then I could forget him completely!'

'Don't say that,' I protested, 'he's a human being. There are worse men than him in the world!'

'He *isn't* human,' she replied. 'I gave him my heart, and he

51

destroyed it, so I can't feel pity for him. But I must tell you how I managed to escape. Hindley Earnshaw should have been at Catherine's burial yesterday, but he had been drinking so much that he couldn't go. Last night he and I were sitting silently in the kitchen at about midnight, when Heathcliff came home. Hindley decided to lock the doors so that Heathcliff could not get in. He told me his plan was to murder his hated guest that night, with the weapon he had shown me. I hate Heathcliff too, but I could not agree to murder, so I called out a warning from the kitchen window. Heathcliff swore horribly at me and broke one of the windows. Hindley put his right arm out through the hole, with the gun in it, and aimed it at his enemy. But before he could fire, Heathcliff caught hold of the gun and pulled it away from Hindley. The knife cut into Hindley's wrist, and blood poured out. Heathcliff jumped into the kitchen through the window, and started kicking and hitting Hindley, who was lying unconscious on the kitchen floor.

'I ran off to find Joseph. When we came back, Heathcliff was putting a bandage on Hindley's wrist. Joseph was shocked at the sight of his master, and would have gone to the police, if Heathcliff hadn't forced me to describe what happened. I had to agree that Hindley had certainly attacked Heathcliff first.

'The next day, I decided to have my revenge on Heathcliff, by telling Hindley that 'that devil' had hit and kicked him when he was unconscious. And I told Heathcliff to his face that he could never have made Catherine happy, if she had been his wife. This made him so angry that he threw a knife at me, which cut my neck, and then he rushed towards me, swearing violently. I knew I had to get away quickly, and as I ran out of the kitchen, I saw Hindley attack Heathcliff. Both of them were rolling on the floor, fighting. I came over the moors through the snow to the

Grange. At last I'm free! And I shall never, never spend another night at Wuthering Heights.'

After drinking her tea, Isabella left the Grange. From our village she travelled by coach to the south, where she made her new home near London. There, a few months later, she had a son. She called him Linton.

Heathcliff must have discovered this from the servants. One day when I saw him in the village, he said, 'I hear I've got a son, Ellen, whose name's Linton! I suppose Isabella wants me to hate him! She can keep him for the moment. But tell Edgar Linton I'll have the boy one day! He's mine!'

After Catherine's death my poor master, Mr Edgar, was a changed man. He no longer went to church, or saw any friends. He occasionally went for lonely walks on the moors, and regularly visited his wife's grave. But fortunately Catherine had left him something of herself, her daughter Cathy. This tiny child soon won his heart.

It's strange, Mr Lockwood, to compare Hindley and Edgar. They both lost their wives, and were left with a child. Hindley did not believe in God, and showed no interest in his son Hareton. But Edgar believed, and loved his daughter Cathy deeply.

Hindley himself died six months after his sister Catherine. We never discovered exactly what happened, but Heathcliff said he had drunk himself to death. It appeared that Heathcliff had won Hindley's house, land and money from him when playing cards, so *he* was now the master of Wuthering Heights. Hareton inherited nothing from his father, and could only stay on at Wuthering Heights as a servant, working for the man who had been his father's enemy.

CHAPTER 12

Bringing up Cathy

———— DURING THE NEXT twelve years I was happier than I
1797 had ever been before. All my time was spent looking
———— after little Cathy, who brought sunshine into our lives.
She was a real beauty, with the Earnshaws' dark eyes and the
Lintons' fair skin. She wasn't as proud and quick-tempered as
her mother, but she was used to getting what she wanted. Her
father loved her so much that he gave her everything, and never
scolded her.

Until she was thirteen she had never been outside the Grange
garden alone. She knew nothing of Wuthering Heights or
Heathcliff. She often asked me about the hills in the distance,
beyond the moors, and wanted to ride her pony there. I knew
the master would not let her leave the safety of the Grange to go
so far, especially as the road to the hills passed close to
Wuthering Heights. So I always told her she would be able to go
there when she was older. I did not know what she was
planning.

Mr Edgar received a letter from his sister Isabella. She wrote
that she was dying of a fever, and asked him to visit her for the
first and last time. She also wanted him to take care of her son
Linton after her death. Although my master hated travelling, he
did not hesitate to do as she requested. He told me to look after
Cathy carefully, and left at once.

He was away for three weeks. Cathy did not cause me any
trouble at first. She spent her days walking her dogs and riding
her pony in the large garden. But one day she asked if she could

stay out the whole day, and away she went on her little pony, with her two dogs running behind.

There was no sign of her at tea-time, and I began to be seriously worried. I went outside to look for her. At the gate I found a workman, who had seen her jump the low wall separating the garden from the road, and then ride on towards the hills and Wuthering Heights.

I was very frightened now. She could be lost on the moors! She could have tried to climb the hills, and fallen! I walked across the moors as fast as I could, and arrived breathless at Wuthering Heights. How glad I was to see one of her dogs lying outside the kitchen door! I knocked loudly, and Zillah let me in. I knew she had been the housekeeper there since Hindley's death.

'Ah,' she said, 'you've come for your little mistress! She's here, quite safe! The master, Mr Heathcliff, isn't here. He won't be back for a while.'

Cathy was sitting comfortably in the kitchen, talking eagerly to Hareton. He was now a big, strong young man of eighteen, who was staring rather stupidly at her. I was delighted to find her again, but I pretended to be angry to punish her.

'Well, miss! You *are* wicked, going such a long way all alone! I've been all over the moors looking for you! Your father will be angry!'

'What have I done?' she sobbed, suddenly frightened. 'Father didn't forbid me to leave the Grange garden! He won't scold me, Ellen. He's never cross, like you! And I've been to the hills, Ellen! This – man – showed me, because I didn't know the way.'

I made her put on her hat and prepare to leave.

'Whose house is this?' she asked suddenly. 'It's *your* father's, isn't it?' she added, turning to Hareton.

'No,' he replied, looking down. His face went very red.

'Whose then – your master's?' she asked.

He swore, and turned away.

'Ellen, he didn't say "miss" to me. Servants should always say "miss", shouldn't they?'

Hareton frowned and looked very angry, but said nothing.

'You, get my horse,' she ordered him. 'Hurry!'

'What the devil do you mean? I'm not your servant!' he growled.

'You see, Miss Cathy? Nice words to be used to a young lady! Now come along, let's fetch the pony and leave,' I said.

'But Ellen,' she cried, staring horrified at him, 'how dare he speak to me like that! He must do as I tell him!'

'He's not your servant, miss,' said Zillah, who had been listening to the conversation. 'He's your cousin.'

'*He* can't be *my* cousin!' cried Cathy, with a scornful laugh. 'Father has gone to fetch my cousin from London. He's a gentleman's son, not – not a farm worker like him!' She pointed at poor Hareton, whose clothes were old and dirty.

I was very annoyed with her and Zillah. Now Heathcliff would hear about his son's arrival, which we had hoped to keep secret from him. And Cathy would certainly ask her father whether she had a cousin at Wuthering Heights. On our way home I explained to her that if her father discovered she had visited Wuthering Heights, he would perhaps be so angry with me that he would send me away. She could not bear to think of that, so she promised to keep her visit a secret from him.

We heard from Mr Edgar that his sister had died, and that he was returning soon with his young nephew. Cathy was wild with excitement. She would see her dear father again, and have a cousin of the same age to play with.

But when the coach arrived, young Linton had to be carried into the house. He was a pale, thin boy, who looked very like Mr Edgar. He seemed so weak that I wondered how long he would live. I thought he would have no chance of life if his father Heathcliff took him to live at Wuthering Heights.

In fact Linton only stayed one night with us. Later that evening Heathcliff's servant Joseph arrived and asked to speak to the master. Although it was late and Mr Edgar was tired after his journey, Joseph insisted, so I took him to the master's room.

'Heathcliff has sent me for his son, and I can't go back without him,' he said.

Mr Edgar was silent for a moment. On his face was an expression of deep sadness. He had hoped to keep Linton with him, as Isabella had wished. But he could not refuse the boy's father.

'Tell Mr Heathcliff,' he said calmly, 'that Ellen will take his son to Wuthering Heights tomorrow. He's asleep at the moment, and I won't disturb him.'

'No!' said Joseph, banging the table with his hand. 'I must take him back now!'

'Not tonight!' answered Mr Edgar. 'Leave the house now, and tell your master what I said!'

'Very well!' shouted Joseph, as he walked out. 'If he doesn't arrive early in the morning, Heathcliff will come for him!'

CHAPTER 13

Heathcliff's son at Wuthering Heights

_____ LINTON WAS VERY surprised to be woken so early,
1797   and told that he had another journey to make, before
_____ breakfast. As we rode the four miles to Wuthering
Heights, he kept asking me questions about his new home, and
the father he had never seen. When we arrived, Heathcliff,
Hareton, and Joseph all came out of the house to inspect the
child.

'Master, that's not a boy,' said Joseph after a while. 'Look at
that white skin and fair hair! Mr Edgar's sent you his daughter
instead!'

'God! What a beautiful creature!' laughed Heathcliff
scornfully. 'That's worse than I expected!'

I helped the trembling child off the horse and into the house.
Heathcliff took him roughly by the arm.

'I hope you'll be kind to him, Mr Heathcliff,' I said. 'He's
weak, and ill. And he's all the family you've got!'

'Don't worry, Ellen,' replied Heathcliff with a smile. 'As
Isabella's son he'll inherit Thrushcross Grange one day, and I
don't want him to die before that. He'll be educated as a
gentleman. But I'm bitterly disappointed at having such a weak,
crying baby for a son!'

So poor Linton was left in his father's care. At first Cathy was
miserable, because she would not now have anyone to play
with, but she soon forgot him. Whenever I met Zillah, the
housekeeper, in the village, I used to ask her about Linton.

'He's often ill,' she told me. 'And so selfish! He has to have a fire even in summer! He calls for cakes and hot drinks all the time. He only ever thinks of himself. Mr Heathcliff can't bear being in the same room as him!'

Several years passed without any more news of Linton. In 1800 Cathy reached the age of sixteen. We never celebrated her birthday, because it was also the day her mother died. On this particular day she came downstairs, dressed for going out, and suggested a walk on the moors with me. Her father gave permission.

It was a lovely spring morning, and I was very happy walking in the sunshine, watching Cathy running ahead of me. But we had walked further than I had realized, and I called to her to come back. She did not seem to hear me. We were on the moors, close to Wuthering Heights, when I caught sight of two men talking to her. I recognized Heathcliff and Hareton at once. I hurried to catch up with her.

'Miss Cathy,' I said breathlessly, 'we must go home. Your father will be getting worried.'

'No, he won't, Ellen. This gentleman wants me to go to his house and meet his son. He says we've already met, but I don't remember, do you? Let's go, Ellen!'

Although I protested, she and Hareton were already halfway to Wuthering Heights. Heathcliff and I followed behind.

'It's very bad of you, Mr Heathcliff,' I scolded him. 'Mr Edgar will blame me for letting her go to your house.'

'I want her to see Linton, Ellen,' he replied. 'Listen to my plan. It's really a very generous one. I want the two cousins to fall in love and marry. You know Cathy won't inherit anything from her father. My son Linton will inherit all the Linton fortune when Edgar dies. If she marries Linton, she'll be wealthy. Of course, if Linton dies, then the money comes to me,

We were on the moors, close to Wuthering Heights,
when I caught sight of two men talking to her.

as his only other relation.'

I was still angry with Heathcliff, but it was too late to stop Cathy entering Wuthering Heights. She was delighted to rediscover her cousin Linton, who was keeping warm by the fire.

'If he is my cousin, and you are his father,' she said to Heathcliff, smiling, 'then you must be my uncle! Why don't you ever visit us at the Grange?'

'I visited it once or twice too often before you were born,' he said. 'I must tell you that I quarrelled violently with your father

60

once. He hates me, and if you tell him you want to come here, he'll forbid it.'

'Well, if I can't come here, Linton can come to visit me at the Grange,' suggested Cathy happily.

'It'll be too far for me,' said her cousin weakly. 'It would kill me to walk four miles.'

Heathcliff looked scornfully at his son.

'I don't think my plan will ever succeed, Ellen!' he whispered to me. 'Who would fall in love with a selfish baby like that?' He went to the kitchen door and called, 'Hareton! Come and take Miss Cathy round the farm.' Cathy was eager to see the animals, and she and Hareton went out.

As we watched them through the kitchen window, Heathcliff seemed to be thinking aloud.

'I've taken my revenge on his father, by making Hareton work for me. I treat him badly, as they used to do to me, and he suffers, as I used to. He's intelligent, and strong, and handsome, but I've taught him to scorn those qualities. So now he's just an uneducated farm worker, and knows nothing of the world. That's how he'll always be. And my son? He's stupid, and weak, and ill. But he's a gentleman, and he'll marry Cathy, and he'll be rich!'

Meanwhile Linton had got up from his armchair and gone out to join Cathy and Hareton. Through the open window I could hear the two younger ones laughing at Hareton's coarse way of speaking. I began to dislike Linton rather than pity him.

When we arrived back at the Grange, Cathy told her father about the visit. He did not want to frighten her, and, in my opinion, did not explain clearly enough why she should never communicate with Linton again. At the time she seemed to accept her father's wish.

During the next few weeks, however, I noticed Cathy's behaviour change. She was always writing on little pieces of paper, which she kept in a locked drawer in her room, and every morning she got up surprisingly early to go down to the kitchen. I suspected something, and one day I decided to break open her drawer. In it I was horrified to find a whole pile of love letters from Linton. The two cousins had been writing to each other in secret for several weeks, and Cathy had used the milkman as a messenger. I told her at once that I knew her secret, and made her promise not to send or receive any more letters. We burnt Linton's letters together.

CHAPTER 14

Secret visits

——— THE MONTHS PASSED, and soon it was autumn. Mr
1800 Edgar caught a bad cold, which seemed to get worse
——— and worse. He stayed indoors the whole winter, so
Cathy only had me as a companion on her walks. She had become very quiet and sad since her relationship with Linton had ended, and was very worried about her father's illness. One day when we were walking in the Grange garden, I noticed her crying.

'Cathy, what's the matter, love?' I asked.

'Oh, Ellen,' she sobbed, 'what shall I do if Father dies? And if you die? I'll be left alone!'

'I hope he and I have years more of life ahead of us. All you need do is look after your father, and let him see you're cheerful.

But I think he would be really ill if he thought you loved Linton, whose father would like to see Mr Edgar dead.'

'I'll never, never do anything to worry or annoy Father,' she promised. 'I only want him to recover. I love him more than anyone else in the world, more than myself!'

Just then we reached the gate, and I saw a gentleman on a horse looking over it. It was Heathcliff.

'Miss Linton!' he called. 'There's something I must tell you!'

'I won't listen,' answered Cathy. 'Father and Ellen both say you're a wicked man.'

'But this is about my son Linton, not me. What a trick you played on him! You wrote him all those love letters, and then I suppose you got tired of it, and stopped! Well, you've broken poor Linton's heart. I swear, he's dying of love for you, and he'll be in the grave by next summer unless you help him! Be generous, come and visit him. I'll be away all next week, so your father won't be angry if you come.'

He rode away. Although I tried to persuade Cathy that Heathcliff could not be telling the truth, my young mistress was very upset, and determined to discover how Linton was.

The next morning we rode to Wuthering Heights. We found Linton alone, lying on a sofa. He looked feverish and ill, and had a bad cough.

'Will you shut the door?' he said crossly, as we entered. 'It's so cold! No, Cathy, I can't breathe if you kiss me! I want a drink.'

Cathy poured him a glass of water.

'And are you glad to see me, Linton?' she asked hopefully.

'Yes, I am,' he replied. 'But you should have come before! My father swore at me, and said it was my fault you didn't come. Will you come and visit me again?'

'Yes, Linton,' Cathy said gently, holding his hand. 'If Father

'Are you glad to see me, Linton?'

agreed, I'd spend half my time with you. I wish you were my brother, then we could spend all our time together!'

'But my father says you would love me best if you were my wife, so that would be better.'

'I'd never love anybody more than Father,' she replied seriously. 'Sometimes men hate their wives, like your father. He hated your mother, my aunt Isabella. That's why she left him.'

'That's not true!' cried the boy. 'Anyway, *your* mother hated *your* father! And she loved mine!'

'You're lying! I hate you!' she shouted angrily, and gave the sofa a violent push. He fell back, and started coughing so badly that even I was frightened. At last he recovered. Cathy was crying in a corner, afraid that she had really hurt him.

'How do you feel now, Linton?' she asked after a while. 'I'm sorry, I didn't mean to hurt you.'

'I wish you felt as ill as I do, you cruel thing! And I was better today, before you came!' His voice was full of pity for himself.

'We must go,' I said. 'You can see, Miss Cathy, that he isn't dying of love for you! It's not your fault that he's ill. Come along!' But I could not stop Cathy whispering something in Linton's ear, before we left the room.

On the way home I told her I would not allow her to visit him again.

'He's a selfish child, Miss Cathy, and I don't think he'll live till he's twenty. I'm glad you're not going to marry him.'

Cathy looked sad. 'I'm sure he'd recover if *I* looked after him. And I don't think we'd quarrel if we knew each other better.'

'Well, miss, if you try to go there again, with or without me, I'll tell your father.'

But the next day I fell ill, and had to stay in bed for three weeks, which was very unusual for me. My little mistress went from her father's bedroom to mine, and back again, and looked after us both with the greatest care. But I never wondered what she did in the evenings, when Mr Edgar had gone to bed, and I no longer needed her.

I only discovered the truth on the first day I was able to get up. In the evening I asked her to read to me, and was surprised how sleepy she seemed. She went to bed early. I felt rather worried about her health, and went to her room an hour later to see if she needed anything. Her bedroom was empty. I sat there in the dark, waiting for her to return.

When she arrived, shaking the snow off her shoes, she was shocked to find me there. I guessed where she had been, but I made her tell me the whole story. Every night since I had been ill, she had ridden to Wuthering Heights and spent the evening with her cousin. Sometimes she was happy with Linton, when he was cheerful and less selfish, but most of the time she was miserable. However, she insisted that the visits should continue, because Linton needed her, and she wanted to see him.

Although she begged me to say nothing to her father, I went straight to the master and told him. He forbade her to visit Wuthering Heights again. She had to obey her father, although it made her very sad.

Well, Mr Lockwood, all this happened only about a year ago. I never thought I would be telling a stranger this story! But who knows how long you'll be a stranger? You're too young to live alone for long, and no one could see Cathy and not love her. Anyway, I'll continue my story.

CHAPTER 15

A trap

A FEW DAYS after the master had forbidden Cathy to

1800   visit Linton, he asked my opinion of the boy.

'Tell me honestly, Ellen, what do you think of his character?'

'Well, sir, I don't think he's wicked, like his father. But you'll have plenty of time to get to know him, sir. He's too young to marry yet.'

Mr Edgar walked to the window and looked out. It was a misty February evening, but the churchyard was just visible.

'I've often prayed for death, Ellen. I've been very happy with my little Cathy. But I've been just as happy lying, through the long June evenings, on her mother's grave, and looking forward to the moment when I can join Catherine there! I haven't got much time left, Ellen. What can I do for Cathy before I die? Should she marry Linton? I wouldn't mind him being Heathcliff's son, if only he loved her and could be a good husband to her.'

'God will show us what to do, sir,' I replied.

In the spring Mr Edgar was still ill, and he continued to worry about Cathy's future. One day he wrote to Linton inviting him to visit the Grange. Linton wrote a long letter back, explaining that his father would not allow him to do that. He begged his uncle to let him meet Cathy for a walk or a ride on the moors between the Grange and Wuthering Heights, as they could not meet in either house. Mr Edgar refused at first, and Linton sent him several more letters. I am sure they had all been carefully checked by Heathcliff before they were posted.

Finally Mr Edgar agreed. He hoped that, if Cathy married Linton, who would inherit the Linton fortune, she would at least be able to remain in her family home. He had no idea that Linton was seriously ill. Neither did I. I never imagined that a father could treat a dying child as cruelly and wickedly as we later discovered Heathcliff had done.

It was a hot, sunny day in summer when Cathy and I rode out to meet her cousin. We were both shocked to discover that he could neither ride nor walk, and was lying on the grass, waiting for us. He looked even paler and weaker than the last time I had seen him. During our meeting he did not seem interested in Cathy or her news. Cathy noticed this immediately.

'Well, Linton,' she said after a while, 'you don't want to talk to me, so I think I'll go home.'

'No, no!' he cried, getting quite excited. 'Not yet! Stay – at least another half-hour! My father will be angry with me if you leave early!'

'I suppose we can stay a few minutes longer,' said Cathy.

We waited, talking to each other quietly while Linton slept a little. Sometimes he cried out in pain.

'Do you think his health is better now than before?' whispered Cathy.

'I'm sorry, Miss Cathy, I think it's much worse,' I answered.

Cathy called her pony, and the sound woke Linton up.

'If you see my father,' he said, hesitating, 'could you tell him I've been cheerful? He'll be here soon!' And he looked round in terror.

'I'll be here next Thursday!' cried Cathy, as she jumped on her pony. 'Come on, Ellen!'

In the week that followed, Mr Edgar's illness grew worse

every day. Cathy could not avoid realizing how serious it was, and sat by his bedside day and night, looking sad and pale. Her father's room had become her whole world. On Thursday I thought a ride in the fresh air would be good for her, and Mr Edgar gladly gave her permission to see Linton. He was hoping that she would not be left alone after his death. I did not want to worry him in his last moments, so I did not tell him that Linton was also dying.

We rode on to the moors and found Linton lying in the same place as before. He was looking very frightened.

'I thought you weren't going to come!' he said.

'Why won't you be honest?' cried Cathy at once. 'Why have you brought me here again, if you don't want to see me? My father's very ill and I should be with him.'

Tears rolled down Linton's face. He seemed terrified.

'Oh, I can't bear it!' he sobbed. 'Cathy, I daren't explain! But if you leave me, he'll kill me! *Dear* Cathy, my life is in your hands! Kind, sweet Cathy, perhaps you *will* agree, and then he won't hurt me!'

Cathy was no longer impatient. 'Agree to what, Linton?' she asked gently. 'Tell me everything! You wouldn't do anything to hurt me, would you, Linton? I'm your best friend.'

'I daren't tell you! My father — ' the boy gasped. Just then Heathcliff appeared. He did not look at Cathy and Linton, who continued talking to each other, but he spoke quietly to me.

'Ellen, how is Edgar? Is he dying, as the villagers say?'

'It's true, the master is dying,' I answered.

'That boy over there is dying too. I only hope Edgar dies before him. If Linton dies first, my plan will fail.' He shouted angrily to his son, 'Get up, Linton!' and then said politely to Cathy, 'Miss Cathy, would you help him back to the house.

'That boy over there is dying too.'

He can't walk far alone.'

'Father has forbidden me to enter your house,' said Cathy.

'Well, come along, Linton. *I'll* have to take you home then,' said Heathcliff.

'No! No! No! Please, Cathy! You *must* come with me!' screamed Linton wildly. He held desperately on to her arm.

Cathy could not refuse the boy, who seemed almost mad with fear. So we all walked the few steps to Wuthering Heights. When we had entered the house, however, I was horrified to see Heathcliff lock the front door. The key was in his hand.

'Hareton, Joseph and Zillah are all out of the house,' he said calmly, 'so we are quite alone.'

'Give me that key!' cried Cathy angrily. 'I'm not afraid of you!' She took hold of his closed hand and bit it. He hit her violently several times, on both sides of the head, and she fell into a chair, trembling. I rushed at him, but he pushed me away.

'Cry as much as you like, Miss Cathy,' he said. 'In a few days *I'll* be your father, and I'll punish you just like that, as often as necessary!'

When Heathcliff went out to look for our horses, Cathy and I hurried round the kitchen looking for a way to escape. But all the doors and windows were locked. Linton was sitting calmly in a chair near the fire, happy that *he* was not being punished this time. We persuaded him to explain his father's plan to us.

'Father is afraid I'll die soon, you see, so he wants us to be married tomorrow morning. You'll have to stay here all night, Cathy. Then perhaps he'll let you go home in the morning.'

'*You* marry this beautiful, healthy young lady?' I cried. 'You must be mad! And wicked too! You and your father have tricked us into coming here!' And I shook him until he started coughing.

'I *must* go home *now*. Father will be worried already,' said Cathy. 'I love Father better than you, Linton!'

Heathcliff returned and sent his son upstairs to bed.

'Mr Heathcliff,' begged Cathy, 'Father will be miserable if I don't go home. *Please* let me go. I promise to marry Linton. Father would like it, and I love him. Why do you force me to do something I want to do?'

'He can't force you!' I cried. 'I'll go to the police!'

'To the devil with you, Ellen! Miss Cathy, I'm delighted that your father will be miserable. In that case you will certainly stay here for twenty-four hours. You won't leave here until you've kept your promise to marry Linton.'

'Please send Ellen to let Father know I'm safe!' sobbed Cathy bitterly. 'Poor Father! He'll think we're lost!'

'Your father must have hated you when you came into the world (I did, at least), and he'll hate you as he leaves it. Go on crying. That's what you'll be doing when you're Linton's wife. He'll make a cruel, selfish husband, I think.'

Heathcliff took us upstairs to Zillah's room, where we spent the night, locked in. Neither of us could sleep. At seven the following morning he came to fetch Cathy, and took her away. From that moment I saw nobody except Hareton, who brought me food, for four whole days and nights.

On the fifth morning Zillah came into the room. She was surprised and pleased to see me, and told me the villagers all thought Cathy and I had got lost on the moors, and died, four days ago. I ran out of the room to look for Cathy.

The big kitchen was full of sunshine, and the door was open, but the only person there was Linton.

'Where is she? Where is Miss Cathy?' I cried wildly.

'Upstairs, in a locked room,' he replied calmly, eating a piece of sugar. 'We won't let her go yet. Father says I shouldn't be soft with Cathy. We've had the wedding ceremony, so she's my wife now, and must stay with me. I don't care if she cries, or is ill!'

'Have you forgotten her kindness to you last winter, when you wrote that you loved her, and she used to come through wind and snow to see you? Now you believe your father's lies about her! And you leave her alone, ill and crying in a strange house! You pity yourself, but you won't pity her! What a heartless, selfish boy you are!'

'I can't stay with her! She cries so much I can't bear it! I can't sleep with all that noise. She promised that if I gave her the key to our room, she'd give me all her nice books, and her pony, but I told her she had nothing to give. They're all mine, or they'll belong to me very soon. And then she cried, and took a little gold case from around her neck. Inside were two pictures, one of her mother and one of her father. I wanted to take them both from her, but she wouldn't let me, so I screamed for help. My father came, and ordered her to give him the pictures and the case. When she refused, he – he hit her on the face and knocked her down, and broke the gold case under his foot. He took away the picture of her mother.'

'And were you pleased to see Miss Cathy hurt?' I asked.

'My father was right to punish her. But I didn't like seeing her mouth full of blood. She can't speak because of the pain. Now you've made me tired with all this talking! You won't find the key to the room! Go away!'

As there seemed to be no chance of persuading him to help her escape, I decided to go back to the Grange as quickly as possible, and rescue her later.

What a welcome I received from the servants at the Grange, who thought I was dead! But I did not have time to tell them my story. I went straight to my master's room. He was lying in bed, very weak and close to death. I told him how Heathcliff had trapped us, and that Cathy was probably married to Linton by now. Mr Edgar realized that his enemy wanted to get hold of the Linton fortune, through his son. He asked me to send for his lawyer, to make arrangements so that Cathy would not lose all her inheritance.

I did as he asked, but the lawyer sent a message, saying that he could not come until the next day. I also sent four strong men with weapons to Wuthering Heights, to demand my young lady's freedom. I was very angry when they returned without her, because Heathcliff had sent them away.

But I needn't have worried. In the middle of the night, as I was taking some water to the master, I heard a knock on the front door, and went to open it. It was my little mistress!

'Ellen, Ellen!' she sobbed. 'Is Father still alive?'

'Yes,' I cried, 'and thank God you're safe with us again!'

'I managed to make Linton help me escape from the room! Now I must see Father!'

I could not bear to be present at their meeting. I waited outside the bedroom door. But they were both calm. Cathy's despair was as silent as her father's happiness. He died in perfect peace, Mr Lockwood. Kissing her, he whispered, 'I'm going to join *her*, and you, dear child, will join us!' He did not move or speak again.

Cathy did not cry, but sat silently by his dead body all morning. At lunch-time the lawyer arrived, too late to help Cathy. Heathcliff had bribed him to stay away. He gave us Heathcliff's orders. All the servants except me had to leave. Cathy, Mrs Heathcliff now, was only allowed to stay at the Grange until her father was buried.

'I'm going to join her, and you, dear child, will join us.'

CHAPTER 16

Cathy becomes a widow

ON THE EVENING after the burial, Heathcliff came to
1800–1 fetch Cathy.

'Why not let her stay here with me?' I begged.

'I'm looking for someone to rent the Grange from me,' he
answered. 'You'll stay on here as housekeeper, Ellen, but Cathy
must come to Wuthering Heights. From now on she'll have to
work for her food.'

'I *shall* work,' replied Cathy. 'And I'll look after Linton. He's
all I've got to love in the world. I'm just sorry for you, Mr
Heathcliff. *You* have nobody to love you! You are as lonely and
miserable as the devil! *Nobody* will cry for you when you die!
I'm glad I'm not you!'

'Go and get your clothes, you wicked girl,' he said. 'We'll be
leaving in a few minutes.' When she had gone, he walked across
the room to look at the picture of Cathy's mother, Catherine,
which was hanging on the wall.

'Do you know what I did yesterday, Ellen?' he said, turning
quickly away from the picture. 'I went to the churchyard, and
asked the man who was digging Edgar's grave to open the lid of
Catherine's coffin for me. Her face looked just the same! I could
not stop looking at her. When the man closed the lid, I broke
open one side of her coffin, the side away from Edgar's grave,
and covered it up with earth. And I bribed the man to bury me
there when I die, next to her, and to take the side of my coffin
away too, so that *I* shall have her in my arms, not Edgar!'

'You were very wicked, Mr Heathcliff, to disturb the dead!'

'I disturbed nobody, Ellen, and I feel much happier now. *She* is the one who has disturbed *me*. For eighteen years she has haunted me. You know I was wild, almost mad, after she died. For days I prayed for her ghost to return to me. On the day of her burial, I went to her grave in the evening. There was a bitter wind, and snow on the ground. I wanted so much to have her in my arms again! So I dug down through the loose earth to her coffin, and was about to pull the lid off, when I felt a warm breath on my face. She seemed to be with me, not in the earth, but close to me. I was so happy that she was with me again! I filled in the grave, and ran eagerly home to the Heights. I looked impatiently round for her. I could feel her but I could not see her! And since then, she has played plenty of tricks on me like that. When I sleep in her bedroom, I can hear her outside the window, or entering the room, or even breathing close to me, but when I open my eyes, I'm always disappointed. Slowly, slowly, she's killing me, with the ghost of a hope that's lasted eighteen years!'

He was talking almost to himself, so I did not answer. When Cathy came in, he stood up, ready to go.

'Goodbye, Ellen!' whispered my dear little mistress. 'Come and visit me!' As she kissed me, her face felt as cold as ice.

'Oh, no you won't, Ellen!' said Heathcliff. 'I'll send for you if I want you!' and together they left the Grange.

I haven't seen Cathy since then. Once I went to the Heights to visit her, but I was not allowed to see her. About six weeks ago I had a long conversation with Zillah, the housekeeper, who gave me news of Cathy. It appeared that, when she arrived at the Heights, she did her best to look after her sick husband. He was obviously dying, although Heathcliff refused to call the doctor. Only a few weeks after her arrival, Linton died in the night, with only Cathy by his bedside. Heathcliff inherited all of Linton's, and what had been Cathy's, fortune, so Cathy is now very poor.

She must be very miserable, and very lonely, in that dark, unpleasant house. Heathcliff hates her, and Joseph and Zillah don't speak to her, because they think she's too proud. Poor Hareton would like to be friendly with her, but she scorns him because he's uneducated. I would like to leave my job here, rent a little cottage and ask Cathy to come and live with me, but Mr Heathcliff will never permit that. Of course, if she married again, she could leave that house, but *I* can't arrange that.

CHAPTER 17

Mr Lockwood visits Wuthering Heights again

AFTER HEARING THE end of Mrs Dean's story, I made my plans for the future. I decided I did not want to spend another winter at the Grange, and told her I would ride to the Heights to inform my landlord. She handed me a letter to give to Cathy Heathcliff.

1802

When I arrived at the gate, Hareton met me and took me into the house. Cathy was there, preparing vegetables for lunch. She did not bother to greet me.

'She may be beautiful,' I thought, 'but she's not very polite.' I passed by her chair, and cleverly dropped Mrs Dean's note in front of her, so that Hareton wouldn't see it. She, however, just said aloud, 'What's that?'

'A letter from the housekeeper at the Grange,' I said, annoyed with her. She gasped, and tried to pick it up, but Hareton got there first.

'Mr Heathcliff will want to look at this,' he said, putting it in his pocket. But when Cathy pretended to cry, Hareton could not bear to make her sad, and he threw the letter down on the table. She eagerly read every word, and asked me several questions about the people at the Grange.

'Mrs Dean will want an answer to her letter,' I reminded her.

'You must tell her that I have no paper or pens to write with. I haven't even any books!' she answered sadly.

'No books!' I cried. 'How can you manage without them in this lonely place?'

'I always used to read so much that Mr Heathcliff decided to take away my only pleasure and destroy my books. I've looked all over house for them. Joseph only reads the Bible, but some of my books are in Hareton's room! Why did you take them, Hareton? Just because you enjoy stealing? They can't be any use to you!'

'I think Mr Hareton wants to learn,' I said, hoping to prevent a quarrel between them. 'No doubt he took them away to study them.'

'Yes,' replied Cathy, laughing. 'I hear him trying to read to himself sometimes and it's extremely funny! He makes some terrible mistakes!'

After a moment's shocked silence Hareton left the room. He returned almost immediately with his arms full of books, and threw them angrily down at Cathy's feet.

'Take them!' he shouted. 'I never want to see them again!'

'I won't have them now,' she said. 'I'll hate them because they'll make me think of you.'

Hareton picked up the books and threw them on the fire, then walked quickly out of the house.

Mr Heathcliff came in as Hareton went out. He had a restless, anxious expression on his face.

'Mr Heathcliff,' I said, 'I must tell you I'm leaving for London next week, for six months, and I shan't want to rent the Grange any more after October.'

'So, Mr Lockwood, you've got tired of the moors already, have you? Well, have your lunch with Hareton and me, anyway. Cathy, take your lunch in the kitchen with Joseph and Zillah.'

I did not enjoy lunch with my two silent companions, and left the Heights straight afterwards.

'What a pity,' I thought, 'that Cathy Heathcliff and I didn't fall in love, as Mrs Dean would have liked! Then I could have taken her away from this miserable place for ever!'

Several months later, in September, I was travelling to visit friends in Yorkshire. I found myself near Thrushcross Grange, and decided to spend a night there. After all, I was still paying rent for it. When I arrived, I was surprised to find a different housekeeper, who told me Mrs Dean had become housekeeper at the Heights. I wanted to have a walk after travelling all day, so I left orders for the woman to cook my supper and prepare a bedroom for me, and I walked the four miles to Wuthering Heights.

As I came close to the old house, I noticed that there were flowers in the garden, and the doors and windows stood open. I could see two people inside, and I stopped for a moment, curious to hear a little of their conversation.

'Read it again, stupid!' said a voice as sweet as a silver bell. 'Read it correctly this time, or I'll pull your hair!'

'You must kiss me if I get it right.'

'You must kiss me if I get it right,' answered a deep voice. The man was sitting at a table, reading from a book. His handsome face shone with pleasure, and his eyes often left the book to look at the small white hand that lay on his shoulder. The girl stood behind him, bending over to help him. Her face – it was fortunate he could not see her face, or he would never have been able to concentrate on his studies. *I* could see it, and I was bitterly sorry that I had thrown away my chance of seeing that beauty every day of my life.

I did not want to disturb their happiness, so I went round to the back door, where I discovered my old friend Ellen Dean.

'Oh, Mr Lockwood, welcome back!' she cried. 'Are you staying at the Grange again?'

'Yes, Mrs Dean, just for one night. But tell me, why are you housekeeper here now and not at the Grange?'

'Zillah left, you see, and Mr Heathcliff wanted me here.'

'I have a little business with him, about the rent.'

'Oh! Mr Heathcliff is dead, sir. He died three months ago. I manage all Mrs Heathcliff's business for her. She hasn't learnt to do it herself yet, you see.'

'Heathcliff is dead!' I repeated, surprised. 'Well! Tell me how it happened, Mrs Dean!'

'Sit down, sir, and drink some beer. I'll gladly tell you. His life ended very strangely.'

CHAPTER 18

Heathcliff's end

——— I WAS DELIGHTED to come back to the Heights, and
1801–2 hoped I could make Cathy's life more comfortable. But
——— she was restless, and complained of loneliness. At first
she continued to annoy Hareton, by laughing at him, but after a
while she decided she really wanted him as a friend. She
apologized for being rude to him, and offered to teach him
everything she knew. From that moment on, the two cousins

have always been together, studying. Hareton has a lot to learn, and Cathy is not the most patient of teachers. But what they have in common is their love for each other. You see, Mr Lockwood, it was easy enough to win Cathy's heart. But now I'm glad you didn't try. I'll be the happiest woman in England when those two marry!'

Heathcliff noticed little of what was happening around him, and would never have been aware of the cousins' feelings, if it hadn't been for Joseph. In the middle of our lunch one day, the old man rushed into the room, shaking with anger.

'I'll have to leave! I wanted to die here, where I've been a servant for sixty years! But now she's taken my garden from me! She's stolen the boy's soul, master! I can't bear it!'

'Is the fool drunk?' asked Heathcliff. 'Can you explain this, Hareton?'

'I've pulled up two or three of his fruit-trees,' confessed Hareton, 'but I'll put them back again.'

'It was my fault,' added Cathy bravely. 'I asked him to do it. We wanted to plant some flowers there.'

'Who the devil gave you permission?' growled Heathcliff.

'You should let me have a bit of garden, as you've taken all my land!' replied Cathy sharply. 'And you've taken Hareton's land too! He and I are friends now! I'll tell him about you!'

The master stood up, staring at her fiercely.

'Out of the room, wicked girl!' he shouted. 'I'll kill you if I get near you!'

'If you hit me, Hareton will hit you. He won't obey you any more, and soon he'll hate you as much as I do!'

'You'd better leave, Cathy,' whispered Hareton urgently. 'I won't quarrel with Mr Heathcliff.'

But it was too late. I was sure Heathcliff was going to hit her.

He took hold of her, one strong hand in her hair and the other raised over her head. But when he looked into her face, his anger suddenly disappeared, and he let his arm fall to his side. He sat heavily down in his chair and put his hand over his eyes for a moment. We all stared at him.

'You must learn not to make me angry,' he said, trying to be calm. 'Go away, all of you! Leave me alone!' A little later he went out, saying he would return in the evening.

As darkness fell, Cathy and Hareton were busy at their studies in the kitchen. I was sitting with them, happy to see them helping each other so well. I feel they're almost my children, Mr Lockwood, and I'm very proud of them. As the master entered the house, he had a full view of us three. They lifted their eyes to meet his. Perhaps you haven't noticed it, but their eyes are very similar, and they are exactly like those of Catherine Earnshaw. Mr Heathcliff stopped and stared, then looked away. At a sign from me, Cathy and Hareton went quietly out into the garden, leaving me alone with Mr Heathcliff.

'It's silly, isn't it, Ellen,' he muttered, 'that I have worked all my life to destroy these two families, the Earnshaws and the Lintons. I've got their money and their land. Now I can take my final revenge on the last Earnshaw and the last Linton, I no longer want to! There's a strange change coming in my life. I'm in its shadow. I'm so little interested in daily events that I even forget to eat and drink. I don't want to see those two, that's why I don't care if they spend time together. *She* only makes me angry. And *he* looks so like Catherine! But everything reminds me of Catherine! In every cloud, in every tree I see her face! The whole world reminds me that she was here once, and I have lost her!'

'You don't feel ill, sir, do you? Are you afraid of death?'

'I'm not ill, Ellen, and I'm not afraid to die. But I can't continue like this! I have to remind myself to breathe – almost to remind my heart to beat! I have a single wish, for something my whole body and heart and brain have wanted for so long! Oh God! It's a long fight! I wish it were finished!'

For some days after that, Mr Heathcliff avoided meeting us at meals. He ate less and less. Late one night I heard him leave the house. He did not return until the morning. When he came in, I noticed a change in his expression. There was a strange, wild happiness in his face, although he was pale and trembling.

'Will you have some breakfast, sir?' I asked.

'No, I'm not hungry,' he answered.

'I don't think you should stay outside at night, sir. You'll catch a bad cold or a fever!'

'Leave me alone, Ellen,' he replied.

I began to worry about him. He was strong and healthy, but a man must eat in order to live. For the next three days he ate nothing. At every meal the food lay untouched on the plate in front of him. He did not look at the food, or at us. He seemed to be looking at something quite close to him, something we could not see. His fierce black eyes followed it with such eager interest that he sometimes stopped breathing for as much as half a minute.

He did not sleep either. For three days he had spent the night in Catherine Earnshaw's old bedroom, and I could hear him walking up and down, and talking, calling, crying all night.

One morning I managed to speak to him, and make him listen to me. 'Mr Heathcliff, you must have some food and sleep. Look at yourself in the mirror! You look ill and tired.'

'It's not my fault that I can't eat or rest. You wouldn't tell a drowning man to rest when he can see the shore! I'm close to what I've wanted for eighteen years, very close! But my soul's happiness is killing my body!'

'It's a strange kind of happiness, master. Take my advice, and pray to God to forgive you for what you've done wrong in the past, if you think you're going to die.'

'Thank you, Ellen, you've reminded me of something. It's the way I want to be buried. My coffin will be carried to the churchyard in the evening. You and Hareton will be present, nobody else. And make sure my orders about the two coffins are obeyed! I want no ceremony, or words from the Bible – I don't believe in any of that.'

He spent the next night, and the next day, in Catherine's room, muttering and sobbing all the time. I sent for Dr Kenneth, but the door was locked, so the doctor could not see him. The following night was very wet, and in the morning as I walked in the garden, I noticed that the bedroom window was wide open.

'He must be very wet if he's in bed,' I thought, 'the bed is so close to the window. I'll go and look.' I found another key which fitted the lock, and opened the door. Mr Heathcliff was there in bed, lying on his back. His eyes were staring at me, so eagerly and fiercely, and he seemed to be smiling! His face and clothes were wet from the rain, and he did not move. I realized he was dead!

I closed the window. I combed his long, black hair from his forehead. I tried to close his eyes, but they would not shut. Suddenly frightened, I called for Joseph. The old servant came at once, but refused to touch the body.

'Ah, the devil's taken his soul! I warned him that would happen!' he cried. 'You see how wicked he is, smiling at death! But thank God Hareton Earnshaw will have the house and land

86

now, that he should have inherited from his father!' And he went down on his knees to pray.

Hareton was, in fact, the only one who was sad at Heathcliff's death. He and I were present at the burial. Heathcliff was buried next to Catherine's grave, as he had wished. As we were not sure of his age or anything else about him, there is only one word on his gravestone – Heathcliff. The villagers are very frightened of his ghost. They say he often haunts the churchyard and the moors.

Hareton and Cathy will be married on New Year's Day, and they'll move to the Grange. I'll be their housekeeper. Joseph will take care of Wuthering Heights, but most of the rooms here won't be used again.

You'll pass the churchyard, Mr Lockwood, on your way back to the Grange, and you'll see the three gravestones close to the moor. Catherine's, the middle one, is old now, and half buried in plants which have grown over it. On one side is Edgar Linton's, and on the other is Heathcliff's new one. If you stay there a moment, and watch the insects flying in the warm summer air, and listen to the soft wind breathing through the grass, you'll understand how quietly they rest, the sleepers in that quiet earth.

GLOSSARY

bear *(v)* to suffer pain or unhappiness

Bible the holy book of the Christian religion

brain the part of our head that thinks, remembers and feels

brain fever a serious illness of the brain

candle a round stick of wax which burns to give light

churchyard ground near a church where dead people are buried

coffin a long box in which a dead body is placed before burial

cough *(v and n)* to push out air violently and noisily through the throat

darling a friendly or loving word for someone who is dear to you

despair *(v)* to lose all hope; *(n)* a feeling of hopelessness

devil a wicked person, or the opposite of God; **what the devil . . .?** a rude or angry way of asking a question

feeling an emotion (e.g. love, hate, fear)

fever an illness which makes the body very hot

gentleman a man of good family, usually wealthy

gipsy a member of a race of travelling people

growl *(v)* to make a low, threatening sound (such as a dog makes), usually expressing anger

haunt *(v)* (of a ghost) to revisit people or places the person knew when alive

housekeeper a person employed to manage a house

howl *(v)* (of a wind) to blow loudly; (of a person) to give a long, sad cry

landlord a man who owns a house, where other people pay to live

library a room in a house used for reading

maid a girl or woman servant

master a man who employs servants

88

moors a wide, open, often high area of land, covered with rough grass

mutter *(v)* to speak in a low voice that is hard to hear

pale with a white face

pity *(v)* to feel sorry for someone; *(n)* a sympathetic understanding of another person's unhappiness

pony a small horse usually ridden by a child or young person

pray to speak to God

quarrel *(v and n)* to disagree and argue strongly with someone

quick-tempered of someone who gets angry very quickly

recover to get better after an illness

relationship the feelings (e.g. loving) or connection (e.g. master–servant) between two people

scold *(v)* to speak angrily to someone because they have done something wrong

scorn *(v)* to feel or show that you think someone is worthless

servant a person who is paid to do housework

sob *(v)* to cry loudly and very unhappily

soul the part of us which some people believe does not die

sour *(adj)* bitter, unpleasant

suffer to feel pain or sadness; *(n)* **suffering**

swear to promise something very seriously; or to use bad language

treat *(v)* to act or behave towards a person

wicked evil; of bad character

windswept (of a place) exposed to frequent strong winds

ACTIVITIES

Before Reading

1 **Read the back cover and the story introduction on the first page, and choose the most probable answers to these questions.**

1 What kind of trouble does the small, dark child cause?
  a) He makes the Earnshaws quarrel, and dislike each other.
  b) He steals the family's money.
  c) He destroys the family's good name.
  d) He makes everybody afraid of him.

2 What do you think the words 'wuthering heights' mean?
  a) the worst winter weather
  b) a windswept house on a hill
  c) hills where the wind blows fiercely
  d) a rainy place

3 What do you think this story is going to be about?
  a) people with strong, sometimes violent, feelings
  b) young lovers who find happiness together
  c) the effect of bad weather on people's lives
  d) devilish crime and wickedness

2 **Several of the relationships in this story fail. Which character weaknesses do you think are most destructive to a relationship? Put the list below in order, 1 to 12 (1 for the most destructive).**

bad temper	greed	pity	scornfulness
cruelty	jealousy	pride	selfishness
dishonesty	meanness	rudeness	wickedness

91

While Reading

Read Chapters 1 and 2. What do you think you will find out about these people? Choose Y (Yes) or N (No) for each sentence.

1 Heathcliff had been in love with Catherine Earnshaw. Y/N
2 Heathcliff wanted to marry Catherine, but she refused him. Y/N
3 Edgar Linton, Catherine's husband, had treated her badly. Y/N
4 Heathcliff had loved his son very much. Y/N
5 Cathy and Hareton Earnshaw were cousins. Y/N

Read Chapters 3 to 6. Who said this, and to whom? What or who were they talking about?

1 'Look what I've brought you!'
2 'I expect *they* are good children and don't need to be punished.'
3 'How funny and black and cross you look!'
4 'He'll be sorry he's treated me like this!'
5 'What can you talk about? How can you amuse me?'
6 'You've made me afraid and ashamed of you.'
7 'You nearly killed your own son!'
8 'He'll never know how I love him.'

Before you read Chapter 7, can you guess what happens?

1 Will Edgar and Catherine's marriage be a happy one?
2 What will happen to Hindley and his son Hareton?
3 When will Heathcliff return, and what will he do then?

If you were Heathcliff, what would *you* do now?

Read Chapters 7 to 11. Are these sentences true (T) or false (F)? Rewrite the false sentences with the correct information.

1 Edgar and Catherine lived happily together for four years.
2 Edgar was delighted to accept Heathcliff as Catherine's friend.
3 Heathcliff fell in love with Isabella.
4 Isabella would never inherit the Linton fortune.
5 Catherine quarrelled with Heathcliff about Isabella.
6 Edgar told Catherine to choose between him and Heathcliff.
7 Catherine was just pretending to be ill.
8 Isabella was happy with her husband.
9 Hindley Earnshaw was planning to kill Heathcliff.
10 Heathcliff forced Ellen to arrange a meeting with Catherine.
11 Catherine was looking forward to dying.
12 Catherine died in Heathcliff's arms.
13 Heathcliff sent Isabella to London to have her baby.
14 Hindley was murdered by Heathcliff.

Before you read Chapter 12, can you guess the answers to these questions?

1 Will Heathcliff find his son, Linton, and bring him back to Wuthering Heights?
2 Will Heathcliff force Isabella to return to him?
3 Will Edgar remarry?
4 How will Catherine's death affect Heathcliff?
5 Will Cathy grow up to be like her mother?
6 Will the three cousins, Cathy, Linton, and Hareton, ever meet? What will happen if they do?
7 Will Heathcliff be punished for his cruel treatment of Isabella and his violence towards Hindley? If so, how?

93

Read Chapters 12 to 16. Choose the best question-word for these questions, and then answer them.

What / Why

1 . . . did Isabella ask Edgar to visit her in London?
2 . . . was Cathy surprised to learn that Hareton was her cousin?
3 . . . was Heathcliff's opinion of his son when he met him?
4 . . . did Heathcliff treat Hareton so badly?
5 . . . did Cathy do while Ellen was ill in bed?
6 . . . did Heathcliff want Cathy to marry Linton?
7 . . . did Heathcliff do to make sure the marriage happened?
8 . . . was Cathy so desperate to get back to the Grange?
9 . . . did Heathcliff do in the churchyard?

Before you read Chapter 17, what do you think will happen in the end? Choose Y (Yes) or N (No) for each of these ideas.

1 Cathy will escape, and run away to London. Y/N
2 In his despair, Heathcliff will kill himself, and then Wuthering Heights will belong to Hareton. Y/N
3 Cathy will marry again. Y/N

Read Chapters 17 and 18, and answer these questions.

1 Why did Hareton give Ellen Dean's letter back to Cathy?
2 Why was Cathy scornful of Hareton?
3 What did Mr Lockwood see through the window at Wuthering Heights when he returned to Yorkshire some months later?
4 Why did Hareton pull up some of Joseph's fruit-trees?
5 Why didn't Heathcliff take his final revenge?
6 What was Heathcliff's last single wish?
7 How did Heathcliff die?

94

After Reading

1 Who married who in this story? Complete the family trees with the right names.

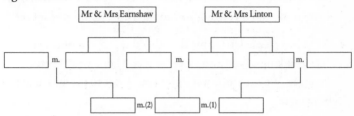

2 There were five weddings and ten deaths in the story. Fill in the names, in the order in which the marriages or deaths happened.

WEDDINGS

1 _____
2 _____
3 _____
4 Cathy & Linton
5 _____

DEATHS

1 _____
2 Frances
3/4 _____
5 _____
6 _____

7 _____
8 _____
9 _____
10 _____

At the end of the story, only two characters were still alive. Who were they?

3 Here are some passages from different letters. Who wrote each one, and to whom? At what point in the story were they written?

1 My darling, I cannot bear living without you in this cold, empty world. I know you think of me as often as I think of you. I *must* see you again! I shall be waiting in the garden . . .

2 I am sorry to have to ask this of you, but I beg you to come to see me as soon as possible. It will be for the last time, as I know that I do not have much longer to live. There is some family business I must discuss with you before the end comes . . .

3 . . . and I know you are lonely and miserable there. Stay out of the master's way, if you can. Remember – you are free to marry again now, and if you did, you could leave that house for ever.

4 Were you pleased to see me the other day, at your house? I've been thinking of you ever since we met. I hope you're getting stronger. Write to me soon – give your letter to the milkman to bring here!

4 **Do you agree (A) or disagree (D) with these statements about the characters? Explain why.**

1 Heathcliff was truly wicked, with no good qualities.
2 Although Heathcliff is often violent and terrifying, we still feel sympathy for him.
3 Catherine married Edgar for all the right reasons.
4 Hindley was just as bad a person as Heathcliff.
5 Ellen Dean was the nicest person in the story.

5 **What would have happened if Catherine *had* married Heathcliff? Decide which of these ideas you agree with, and explain why.**

1 It would have been a very happy marriage.
2 They would have had a large family of loving children.
3 They would never have had much money.
4 They would have quarrelled all the time, and their marriage would have ended in violence.

6 **When Isabella fell in love with Heathcliff, Catherine tried to persuade her that he was not worth loving (see page 32). Complete Isabella's part of the conversation.**

CATHERINE: Isabella, I must talk to you about Heathcliff.

ISABELLA: _____

CATHERINE: Well, he's always been strong, yes, but handsome? No, I wouldn't call him that.

ISABELLA: _____

CATHERINE: That's what I wanted to talk to you about. You *shouldn't* love him. He isn't worth it!

ISABELLA: _____

CATHERINE: Well, he can be very violent, and fierce, and even cruel. There's a certain wildness in him—

ISABELLA: _____

CATHERINE: Me? In love with him? No, no, I'm not, although I'm very close to him. He's almost part of me. But he'd be a bad husband for you, Isabella!

ISABELLA: _____

CATHERINE: Well, yes, it's true that Edgar and I don't want you to marry Heathcliff. You wouldn't be happy with him.

ISABELLA: _____

CATHERINE: I'm sure because – because you and he are so different. You're quiet and gentle and weak, while he—

ISABELLA: _____

CATHERINE: Selfish? Why do you say that?

ISABELLA: _____

CATHERINE: That simply isn't true! It doesn't matter to me whether Heathcliff gets married or not. But I know he won't make you happy.

7 **After Catherine's death, Heathcliff thinks about her more and more as the years pass. Here are his thoughts in the last week of his life. Choose one suitable word to fill each gap.**

What is happening to me? Today, _____ Cathy spoke sharply to me, I _____ my hand to hit her, but _____ prevented me. I looked into her _____ and I saw her eyes – Catherine's _____ eyes! They seem to enter my _____. And Hareton's are the same. I _____ be angry with those two. They _____ me so much of Catherine! But _____ around me tells me that she _____ here once, and that I have _____ her! I'm in darkness, in her _____, and there is nothing, nothing on _____ to live for.

   But recently I've _____ there has been some sort of _____ in me. I feel hot and _____ at the same time. I sometimes _____ to eat or sleep or even _____. I'm closer to Catherine than ever _____! There is just one thing I _____, with all my heart and soul, _____ I've wanted for so long! Catherine, _____ my heartfelt cry of pain! My _____, come back to me! Can't you _____ me with you this time? I'm _____ afraid of death. Our bodies will _____ together in the soft, dark, warm _____, and our souls fly over the _____, together again at last!

8 **The story ends with the two young lovers finding happiness together. Did you like this ending, or would you have preferred a darker ending, such as the ones below? Explain why.**

   1 Heathcliff does take his final revenge, and makes sure that neither Hareton nor Cathy will inherit their parents' houses.
   2 Cathy and Hareton do not fall in love, but continue on the cruel, destructive path that Heathcliff followed for so long.

ABOUT THE AUTHOR

Emily Jane Brontë was born in 1818 in Yorkshire, in the north of England – one of six children of an Irish clergyman, Patrick Brontë, and his wife Maria. By 1825 her mother and two eldest sisters were dead, leaving Emily, her sisters Charlotte and Anne, and their brother Branwell. They were now living in Haworth, a quiet village on the Yorkshire moors, where Emily spent most of her brief life, studying with her sisters, writing stories and poems, and walking on the moors. She had no close friends, wrote few letters, and was never happy away from her home or the wild open moorland she loved so deeply.

In 1846 the three sisters published a book of their poems, using the male pen-names of Currer, Ellis, and Acton Bell. The poems did not sell well, but in 1847 three novels appeared – Emily's *Wuthering Heights*, Charlotte's *Jane Eyre*, and Anne's *Agnes Grey* – and these had much greater success. Meanwhile, at Haworth there were more sad times for the family. Branwell, an alcoholic, died in 1848. In the same year, Emily also died, aged only thirty, and Anne's death followed in July 1849. Only Charlotte was left, to care for her ageing father.

Nineteenth-century readers of *Wuthering Heights*, Emily's only novel, were shocked by the violence of the characters' feelings and actions. Even her sister Charlotte wrote of 'the horror of great darkness' that hangs over the novel. But since then it has become a classic, adapted for the cinema and television; and Emily's writing, both in her novel and her poems, has been described as Shakespearian in its depth and imaginative power.

ABOUT BOOKWORMS

OXFORD BOOKWORMS LIBRARY
Classics • True Stories • Fantasy & Horror • Human Interest
Crime & Mystery • Thriller & Adventure

The OXFORD BOOKWORMS LIBRARY offers a wide range of original and adapted stories, both classic and modern, which take learners from elementary to advanced level through six carefully graded language stages:

Stage 1 (400 headwords)	Stage 4 (1400 headwords)
Stage 2 (700 headwords)	Stage 5 (1800 headwords)
Stage 3 (1000 headwords)	Stage 6 (2500 headwords)

More than fifty titles are also available on cassette, and there are many titles at Stages 1 to 4 which are specially recommended for younger learners. In addition to the introductions and activities in each Bookworm, resource material includes photocopiable test worksheets and Teacher's Handbooks, which contain advice on running a class library and using cassettes, and the answers for the activities in the books.

Several other series are linked to the OXFORD BOOKWORMS LIBRARY. They range from highly illustrated readers for young learners, to playscripts, non-fiction readers, and unsimplified texts for advanced learners.

Oxford Bookworms Starters   *Oxford Bookworms Factfiles*
Oxford Bookworms Playscripts   *Oxford Bookworms Collection*

Details of these series and a full list of all titles in the OXFORD BOOKWORMS LIBRARY can be found in the *Oxford English* catalogues. A selection of titles from the OXFORD BOOKWORMS LIBRARY can be found on the next pages.

David Copperfield

CHARLES DICKENS

Retold by Clare West

'Please, Mr Murdstone! Don't beat me! I've tried to learn my lessons, really I have, sir!' sobs David.

Although he is only eight years old, Mr Murdstone does beat him, and David is so frightened that he bites his cruel stepfather's hand. For that, he is kept locked in his room for five days and nights, and nobody is allowed to speak to him.

As David grows up, he learns that life is full of trouble and misery and cruelty. But he also finds laughter and kindness, trust and friendship . . . and love.

Far from the Madding Crowd

THOMAS HARDY

Retold by Clare West

Bathsheba Everdene is young, proud, and beautiful. She is an independent woman and can marry any man she chooses – if she chooses. In fact, she likes her independence, and she likes fighting her own battles in a man's world.

But it is never wise to ignore the power of love. There are three men who would very much like to marry Bathsheba. When she falls in love with one of them, she soon wishes she had kept her independence. She learns that love brings misery, pain, and violent passions that can destroy lives . . .

The Garden Party and Other Stories

KATHERINE MANSFIELD

Retold by Rosalie Kerr

Oh, how delightful it is to fall in love for the first time! How exciting to go to your first dance when you are a girl of eighteen! But life can also be hard and cruel, if you are young and inexperienced and travelling alone across Europe . . . or if you are a child from the wrong social class . . . or a singer without work and the rent to be paid.

Set in Europe and New Zealand, these nine stories by Katherine Mansfield dig deep beneath the appearances of life to show us the causes of human happiness and despair.

Heat and Dust

RUTH PRAWER JHABVALA

Retold by Clare West

Heat and dust – these simple, terrible words describe the Indian summer. Year after year, endlessly, it is the same. And everyone who experiences this heat and dust is changed for ever.

We often say, in these modern times, that sexual relationships have changed, for better or for worse. But in this book we see that things have not changed. Whether we look back sixty years, or a hundred and sixty, we see that it is not things that change, but people. And, in the heat and dust of an Indian summer, even people are not very different after all.

The Brontë Story

TIM VICARY

On a September day in 1821, in the church of a Yorkshire village, a man and six children stood around a grave. They were burying a woman: the man's wife, the children's mother. The children were all very young, and within a few years the two oldest were dead, too.

Close to the wild beauty of the Yorkshire moors, the father brought up his young family. Who had heard of the Brontës of Haworth then? Branwell died while he was still a young man, but the three sisters who were left had an extraordinary gift. They could write marvellous stories – *Jane Eyre*, *Wuthering Heights*, *The Tenant of Wildfell Hall* . . . But Charlotte, Emily, and Anne Brontë did not live to grow old or to enjoy their fame. Only their father was left, alone with his memories.

Jane Eyre

CHARLOTTE BRONTË

Retold by Clare West

Jane Eyre is alone in the world. Disliked by her aunt's family, she is sent away to school. Here she learns that a young girl, with neither money nor family to support her, can expect little from the world. She survives, but she wants more from life than simply to survive: she wants respect, and love. When she goes to work for Mr Rochester, she hopes she has found both at once. But the sound of strange laughter, late at night, behind a locked door, warns her that her troubles are only beginning.